simply

word

and

spirit

by Ruth Lorensson

First printing in 2016. This 1st edition published 2016 by Upptäcka Press

1918 Constitution Ave
Fort Collins, CO 80526, USA

upptacka.com
@upptacka
info@upptacka.com

© 2016 Ruth Lorensson. All rights reserved. No part of this book may be reproduced in any form or by any electronic or mechanical means including information storage and retrieval systems, without permission in writing from the author or publisher. The only exception is by a reviewer, who may quote short excerpts in a review. The moral right of the author has been asserted.

ISBN 978-0-9571428-1-7

Dedicated to
Chris; my husband, designer and editor. Without you
this book wouldn't exist. Thank you for believing in me.
And Titus & Penny—my hope is that the message of
this book becomes your spiritual inheritance.

In Memory of
Ray Anderson, whose words encouraged
me to write this book.

Deep heartfelt thanks to
Rob and Pam Scott-cook, for demonstrating spiritual
parental wisdom and love to me. David Mitchell, for writing
the foreword for this book, and teaching me so much about
God's heart for local church. Greg and Clare Thompson,
for all the laughs and tears as we chased God's dreams
together. Your lives and ministry continue to inspire me.

contents

foreword	7
introduction	11
1: division	17
2: of the word	33
3: of the spirit	47
4: cornerstone	77
5: indivisible	101
6: passion for the word	163
7: passion for the spirit	205
conclusion	241

foreword

It's a great pleasure to commend this book to you, and to commend its author Ruth to you in the same breath.

'Word & Spirit' are words that belong together; a famous quote I remember from my youth was *'Word without Spirit, dry up; Spirit without Word blow up, Word & Spirit together— grow up'.*

Now no card carrying evangelical would ever admit to a deficient appreciation of the work of the Holy Spirit, similarly no card carrying charismatic would ever admit to being 'unscriptural'. In practice however people or movements that balance these emphases are rare. It can be hard to hold in tension the scholarly pursuit of that 'sound' foundational revelation of scripture alongside an appreciation of and hunger for the 'now' word of prophecy. Evangelicals have been skeptical about spiritual gifts and experiences that may be mystical or trans-rational. Charismatics have been dismissive of or impatient with more conservative members of the Christian family or what they may term as 'old wineskins'.

I believe with Ruth that holding these two in tension is vital for the spiritual health of individuals and churches. Jesus said 'you are in error because you neither know the scriptures or the power of God"[1]. We don't want the lowest common denominator of approaches, we want as much Word and as much Spirit as we can get. The apostles needed both in the first century and I think we need just as much in the twenty-first century. Ruth is a compelling advocate for this approach not least because she lives it. When we worked together in Bristol I would often talk of the importance of 'both and' thinking, and she really wants 'both and' as far as knowing the scriptures and the power of God are concerned!' I hope as you read these pages you sense her passion for Jesus who is revealed in scripture, but also the freshness of a faith where the Spirit is to her indeed a counselor and guide whose presence wells up in the honesty and at times vulnerability of her story.

David Mitchell, Woodlands Church, Bristol.

---

[1] Matthew 22:29

introduction

I seek the will of the Spirit of God through or in connection with the Word of God. The Spirit and the Word must be combined. If I look to the Spirit alone without the Word, I lay myself open to great delusions also.[2]

Nothing but the Blood of Jesus

When I think of my faith as a child, I think of sweet simplicity. Sunday school consisted of bible drills, memory verses and songs for memorizing books of the bible. The main message was *the precious blood of Jesus*. My grandmother used to write letters to me in her 'joined up' (cursive) writing. Always among her tender words of affirmation was her precious scriptures, eloquently written out—treasures of hers that she wanted to pass on to me as an 8-year-old. I was surrounded by people who loved scripture. Bibles were weathered & worn, and brought to prayer meetings, Sunday services and even meal times.

This was the foundation of my faith; a foundation my parents had paved ahead of me. It preceded my more personal walk where I discovered the reality of *friendship with God*, but it's value has never disappeared from my journey. It's no wonder

2 George Mueller, georgemueller.org

that, when the worship leader chooses the old classic *Nothing but the blood of Jesus*, it hits a sweet spot in my heart.

> *What can wash away my sin? Nothing but the blood of Jesus; What can make me whole again? Nothing but the blood of Jesus.*[3]

When we sing it, relief sweeps over me. It centers me. It brings me back to what's important.

When I reflect on these times and people that surrounded me in my early years, I see a quality about the way they treated The Word. It wasn't legalism, it was love; a love for The Word that I rarely glimpse in today's Western Christian culture. A love and passion for The Word that I long to have, that I want to get, save and cultivate.

Finding Friendship with God

I was a young adult when my personal walk with God really began. All the foundational stuff suddenly became reality for me. I met Jesus for myself. When I became a Christian I was introduced to the Holy Spirit who has become my constant friend.

The change from a cultural experience of Christianity to a real relationship with God was a deeply spiritual experience. I had a spiritual dream which changed my life forever.

---

3   Robert Lowery, The United Methodist Hymnal No.362

In the dream my eyes had been opened to the spiritual battle taking place on earth and I was led to an ancient door where I found peace and healing. I wasn't yet a Christian but the dream showed me that I needed to become one – it also showed me my calling and ministry as I continued to show others in this dream the ancient door that I had found.

Such an odd experience, but one that left me in no doubt that God was real, that I was loved and that there is such a thing called salvation.

Although this dream was profoundly spiritual and emotionally charged, my actual experience of becoming a Christian felt fairly normal. It was a few weeks after the dream had occurred, and it weighed deeply in my heart, mind and spirit. Finally on a sunny day while I was visiting Bristol, I quietly invited Jesus into my life forever. I asked for forgiveness. I asked for the Holy Spirit. There were no big fireworks or overwhelming spiritual experiences—just a deep and wonderful peace. I knew something incredibly miraculous had happened, but I felt strangely normal, and it was good.

As I've gone on, one of the most reassuring parts of my journey is the knowledge that I'm not alone. I have a great partner and friend that helps me understand the Father and helps me worship Jesus. He's sustained me, guided me, comforted me, and given me hope & encouragement. He's the one Jesus promised to us—the Holy Spirit. My experience of Him has pushed me past my comfort zone at times, and at others has felt more than natural.

When I reflect on my spiritual walk it's been one where I've experienced the immense value of both the Word & the Spirit. Sometimes I've had seasons where I have relied more heavily on one or the other, but in my heart of hearts, God has put an undeniable passion for both to live in symbiotic harmony.

Why Write this Book?

Firstly, in our Western Christian culture, I believe there's a divide between those with an emphasis on the Word and those with an emphasis on the Spirit. Obviously – as with many issues of division – there are those who don't fall into this category. Some of the most Spirit-led people I know have a deep understanding and passion for the Word, and vice-versa. I'm not wishing to make sweeping statements about the Christian's journey – if you're someone who holds together the Word and the Spirit, I cheer you on and hope you can celebrate this book with me. Still though, there are undeniable pockets within Christ's church that pick a preference.

Secondly – and most importantly – this division matters. Separating the Word and the Spirit grieves the heart of God, stunts Christian growth, hinders Christian mission and restricts the life to the full that Jesus offers.

With this book I hope to draw together these two vital parts of our faith. I aim to unpack what they really mean for us as Christians and encourage a passion for growing in each.

Chapter Synopsis

In Chapter 1 we will take a look at division. Why does this division exist? How damaging is it? Is there anything we can do about it in the church today?

In Chapters 2 and 3 we'll unpack the true meanings of the Word & the Spirit in the hope of getting to the bottom of some of the misunderstandings that fuel the divide.

In Chapter 4 we will center ourselves by looking at the life of Jesus. We'll look at how Jesus – a man of the Word and the Spirit – is the person we should be getting our inspiration from for the Christian life.

In Chapter 5 we'll look at the specific reasons why dividing the Word and the Spirit is so detrimental to the Christian walk.

Finally, in Chapters 6 & 7 we will be looking at how to develop a love for both the Word and the Spirit. We will be forging a new path of unity, spiritual health and growth that will hopefully be a catalyst for many more to receive Jesus.

1
division

All for one and one for all, united we stand divided we fall.[4]

Why does the Church have Division?

The Church has struggled with division since it's earliest days. The Apostle Paul passionately addresses this issue in his letter to the church in Corinth. Interestingly in this case, the church wasn't divided over *doctrine,* but over whom they followed. Labels were created to describe their preference and it was this sub categorization of the Faith that Paul opposed. He was pleading with the Corinthians to hold onto the vital truth that Christ is the only definition needed.

> *I appeal to you, brothers and sisters, in the name of our Lord Jesus Christ, that all of you agree with one another in what you say and that there be no divisions among you, but that you be perfectly united in mind and thought. My brothers and sisters, some from Chloe's household have informed me that there are quarrels among you. What I mean is this: One of you says, "I follow Paul"; another, "I follow Apollos"; another, "I follow Cephas"; still another, "I follow Christ."*

[4] Alexandre Dumas, The Three Musketeers

> *Is Christ divided? Was Paul crucified for you? Were you baptized in the name of Paul?* [5]

Unfortunately, this seed of division and need to qualify the 'type' of Christian continued throughout the ages. The labels changed from generation to generation as more denominations and subcategories of Christianity were established. Christians continued to identify themselves by the names of their leaders, denominations or the aspects of truth they emphasized. *Doctrine, personality* and *the type of Christian experience* continue to divide people today.

When discussing the subject of division it's important to clarify exactly what division is and why it's something Christians should pro-actively disallow in our lives.

Division happens when we get our priorities mixed up. When we choose to be defined by our preferences rather than by our love for one another. Love is the singular attribute that binds Christians together regardless of race, sex, culture or personality—it's supposed to be the hallmark of Christianity. When love is regarded in this way, it has the power to hold a world-wide family of all sorts of people together in the unified representation of Jesus. When love is deprioritized and something else claims first place, we have inadvertently opened the door to division.

There will always be different personalities, doctrines and expressions in God's church. This, on it's own, is not

---

5   1 Corinthians 1:10-13 NIV

division—it's *diversity*.

When diversity of thought, beliefs, personality, style and so on aren't embraced in the church, division occurs.

When we want everyone to be like 'me', when we're frustrated at people who are not like 'me' and when we begin harbor mistrust and sometimes hatred against people who are not like 'me', we inadvertently join the cause of division. The celebration of diversity dwindles as soon as we're on division's side.

What's so Wrong about Division?

> *Every kingdom divided against itself will be ruined, and every city or household divided against itself will not stand.*[6]

Some might say *"So what's the big deal? We've always had division in the church. Maybe that's just the way it is?"*

Jesus certainly didn't think so. His prayer was that we'd be one, that we'd be brought to complete unity.

> *My prayer is not for them alone. I pray also for those who will believe in me through their message, that all of them may be one, Father, just as you are in me and I am in you. May they also be in us so that the world may believe that you have sent me. I have given them the glory that you gave*

---

[6] Matthew 12:25 NIV

> *me, that they may be one as we are one—I in them and you in me—so that they may be brought to complete unity. Then the world will know that you sent me and have loved them even as you have loved me.*[7]

The starting point to understanding *why division in the church is not what Jesus intended* is to remember that, according to the bible, we're supposed to be a family. We're not meant to be an institution or a religious order. The Bible's teaching is clear; that we're a family and God is our Dad. Division in the family simply breaks the Father's heart.

I'm a parent. I have two gorgeous children; Titus (5) and my daughter Penny (2). Even though they look very similar I can tell at this age that they have striking differences in their personalities. I'm sure as they develop their own belief system for life, the universe and God, they won't agree on everything. *Do I want them to be the same?* Of course not—as their mother, I celebrate their differences. *Will I be upset if they don't agree on everything?* No—that's part of them becoming their own persons. *Will my heart break if these differences let the bond of our family break?* Yes—it would break my heart!

The same is true for the church. God the Father isn't wanting us all to be the same. He loves our uniqueness. But He is broken-hearted when we (His kids) argue, hate, separate and disassociate from each other. This knowledge alone is enough for me to hate division too—but it doesn't stop there. Not only does division break the Father's heart, but it makes His

---

7   John 17:20-23 NIV

cause ineffective.

Over the years I've had a number of prophetic dreams which illustrate the ineffectiveness of division and the benefits of unity.

The Two Sisters

A number of years ago I had a striking dream of two sisters who lived together:

> *In this dream there was a big house where two sisters lived and served together. In this house was a great living room where friends would come and spend time together, a huge kitchen where meals were served in abundance and variety, and bedrooms where guests could rest and stay.*
>
> *At some point in the dream, the sisters argued. As they did, a dividing wall was constructed in the middle of the house. Now, instead of the house remaining spacious, it became two small houses under one roof. The houses were very tall and thin due to the fact that they both had to fit into the original house.*
>
> *There were two of everything; two kitchens, two laundry rooms, two front doors and so on. The sisters forgot the wonderful life filled days of the one big house and got used to living with less space.*

This dream was such a noteworthy picture to me of how ineffective and ridiculous the church becomes when division occurs. God's house simply wastes energy by harboring division.

The Bridal Dress

In 2008 I had just begun serving as the prophetic pastor in Woodlands Church. My job was to grow and cultivate a healthy prophetic culture within the church. I remember running my first mid-week training when a handful of excited and skeptical folks turned up eager to see what I was proposing. I was really thrilled to have my friend Abby there—someone I knew was a passionate lover of Jesus and seriously gifted in the prophetic.

That same week I had a prophetic dream that involved myself and Abby buying a wedding dress! The dream went like this:

> *Abby and I were buying a wedding dress together. We were in a bridal shop and went to the counter and said what we wanted. There was a seating area where family and friends of other brides were watching them try on dresses. The others sitting there said to both of us separately "Are you sure this is what you want? Surely you want a dress of your own rather than to share one?" But both Abby and I were resolute that we'd made up our minds, had talked about it beforehand and were sure.*
>
> *Even though we were to share the dress, the dress had certain designs that allowed us both to have a different look. For example the dress was off the shoulder but it had lovely sleeves that could be attached if one of us wanted a long sleeve dress. So in our minds we could buy the same dress yet still have our own look.*

> *As we headed toward the checkout to pay for the dress, we learned that because we were buying the dress together, there was a bonus in store for each of us.*
>
> *For myself, I got bonus store credit. As the woman charged my card she said that Abby had won a free honeymoon to the USA!*

I remember sharing this dream with Abby as she gave me a lift back from church one cold rainy evening. I think for both of us it was profound and had a multi-layered depth of interpretation. It was such a strange dream but I know with all my heart that this dream helped solidify a crucial friendship with Abby who was instrumental in helping me achieve a thriving prophetic ministry within the church. It's also a striking analogy that points to the benefits that come with unity.

Division of Truths as well as People

Division can come from laying an emphasis on a certain truth if that emphasis is not held in context of the big picture. A couple years ago I sensed God speak to me about division and how it was a strategy of Satan. Through dreams and scripture the Holy Spirit highlighted to me how Satan not only tries to divide people, but also God's revelatory truths—like love and holiness. Satan knows the power in God's diverse people working together and the synergy that comes from holding truths together.

People often separate over an emphasis that is laid on a

certain truth that Jesus taught over others.

For example, we have people and movements that focus on *love*. God being love and acting in love is one of the most remarkable bits of knowledge one could ever have. Amazing! But for some people being passionate about this truth means they let go of another; like holiness or the need to be people of truth itself.

Instead of being okay with the mystery and tension that comes with holding together truths like *grace* and *righteousness,* people tend to pick a side and over-emphasize one to the detriment of the other... once again we have a divide. Arguments and squabbles erupt over people who lock themselves into one truth over and above others.

Ironically there are some amazing scriptures that talk about and celebrate the relationship between these chunks of God's revelation. Like Psalm 85:10 where it talks about love, truth, righteousness and peace:

> *Unfailing love and truth have met together. Righteousness and peace have kissed!*

Or in Psalm 89:14 where David talks about the importance of righteousness, justice, love and truth:

> *Righteousness and justice are the foundation of your throne. Unfailing love and truth walk before you as attendants.*

These scriptures reveal an ancient wisdom on how important it is that these aspects of God's kingdom are intertwined.

They're personified as lovers, friends and servants to emphasize the point of their unity. They're meant to all be part of God's church because they are part of God Himself.

My favorite scripture regarding this issue is found in Colossians 1:16-17 where we are given a cosmic vision of Jesus:

> *For in him all things were created: things in heaven and on earth, visible and invisible, whether thrones or powers or rulers or authorities; all things have been created through him and for him. He is before all things, and in him all things hold together.*

The One we are following – the One we are meant to be representing – holds all things together. This is an awesome vision and standard for us to aspire to. Jesus did not pick one thing over another—He masterfully and passionately promoted truths without demeaning others. He held in tension the mysteries of the universe.

The Word and the Spirit are two of these truths that have been divided. Before we unpack them in more detail, let's take a look at the benefits of embracing diversity as God's family on Earth.

The Benefits of Embracing Diversity

> *How good and pleasant it is when God's people live together in unity! It is like precious oil poured on the head, running down on the beard, running down on Aaron's beard, down*

> *on the collar of his robe. It is as if the dew of Hermon were falling on Mount Zion. For there the Lord bestows his blessing, even life forevermore.*[8]

Diversity itself is good. I'm sure you'll agree that we're not all meant to be the same. How boring would that be! Different personalities, preferences and passions are all incredibly important, especially in the church. Without diversity there would be little creativity. Within the church, diversity thrives as much as anywhere else in life.

If you're part of a church I'm sure that if you took a moment it wouldn't be hard to spot the differing personalities and preferences. There are people who are all about 'prayer', there are people who all they can think about is 'mission', we have the 'worshipers', the 'community' folk, those who are passionate about 'justice', the 'practical' people and the 'emotional' people. The list goes on and on.

If we are honest, most of us enjoy being around people who are like us. It's mainly because it makes us feel good about ourselves. It affirms how right our point of view is when we are surrounded by people who share it. There's something natural about that, and that's okay to a point. But if we create church family to be clones of my personality/gifting/passion type, then what we end up doing is severely missing out on God's huge world-view.

We each hold a world-view – a window through which we

---

8   Psalm 133: 1-3 NIV

view life, God and church – but our personal world-views will always be limited. It can be God-given, but it's still limited. When we allow others with a different world-view to love us and influence us, we change, we grow, we become less black and white in our thinking.

The truth is that it's harder work to co-exist and do 'church family' with people who are different. Misunderstandings are common, conflicts can occur and compromise has to be embraced. It makes me smile every time I think about God's plan for church leadership; an apostle, a prophet, a pastor, a teacher and an evangelist! [9] The typical personalities that often go along with these callings are drastically different and are potentially a cocktail for conflict. And yet, in God's wisdom, He puts them together to servant-lead His church. It's worth pondering why He chooses to do this?

I've had first hand experience of this spiritual diversity in my marriage. My husband Chris and I are very different—especially in the way we express our spirituality, thoughts and preferences about church. Chris is completive in his worship and I am more charismatic. Chris prefers small intimate settings to discuss matters on spirituality, but I'm more comfortable with larger expressions. We're very different personalities with very different church backgrounds. We've often said that *either God is having a laugh or it's the work of a master genius.*

Is it hard work? Heck yes – some of our most feisty arguments

---

[9] Ephesians 4:11-13

have been about our differing positions – but with the anchor of our love to each other in place, we've both gained perspective, insight and wisdom that we would not have gained otherwise. Being married to Chris has taught me a huge lesson: that spiritual diversity can be embraced if there is genuine love and friendship, and out of this can come some extraordinary fruit.

At some point we've got to decide what wisdom we believe in. We've got to ask ourselves whether we believe in the importance of diversity and unity. It's certainly easier to split and join groups that are like us. It's only when we believe in the synergy that can happen in diversity that we will be willing to fight for it. Then, we will fight through the fears, misunderstandings and conflict because we know that there's a prize to be won.

Placing Emphasis on Love

We're meant to have passions; things that God has laid specifically on our hearts. I don't think it's humanly possible for one person to fully carry the vision of every area of God's Kingdom. Sometimes just one portion of God's heart and vision demands a lifetime of passion and focus from one person. God has set things apart for us to run with, to carry a torch for; Justice, Healing, Creativity, Mission, The poor, Business and so on. It's when we come together through love that we give the world the full representation of Jesus. That's why, in the gospel of John, Jesus says;

> *By this everyone will know that you are my disciples, if you*

love one another. [10]

It's quite a remarkable verse. Right here in the book of John the common goal, the thing we will be known for and will represent Jesus to every tribe and tongue, the thing we must all guard above all things is *our love of one another*. It's the thing that will – after everything – truly show the whole world that Jesus is the real deal.

I just want to pause on this verse for just a moment. It's a very well known verse. I've preached on it a number of times. It's very easy for us to just nod our heads in agreement with verses like this but we really do need to take stock as it holds a crucial bit of advice for the most important outcome: *everyone getting to see Jesus.*

The commentary from Barnes' Notes on this verse is quite remarkable and challenging:

> *That is, your love for each other shall be so decisive evidence that you are like the Savior, that all people shall see and know it. It shall be the thing by which you shall be known among all men. You shall not be known by special rites or habits; not by a special form of dress or manner of speech; not by special austerities and unusual customs, like the Pharisees, the Essenes, or the scribes, but by deep, genuine, and tender affection. And it is well known it was this which eminently distinguished the first Christians, and was the subject of remark by the surrounding pagans. "See," said*

---

10 John 13:35 NIV

the pagan, "see how they love one another! They are ready to lay down their lives for each other." Alas! how changed is the spirit of the Christian world since then! Perhaps, of all the commands of Jesus, the observance of this is that which is least apparent to a surrounding world. It is not so much that they are divided into different sects, for this may be consistent with love for each other; but it is the want of deep-felt, genuine love toward Christians even of our own denomination; the absence of genuine self-denial; the pride of rank and wealth; and the fact that professed Christians are often known by anything else rather than by true attachment to those who bear the same Christian name and image. The true Christian loves religion wherever it is found equally in a prince or in a slave, in the mansion of wealth or in the cottage of poverty, on the throne or in the hut of want. He overlooks the distinction of sect, of color, and of nations; and wherever he finds a man who bears the Christian name and manifests the Christian spirit, he loves him. And this, more and more as the millennium draws near, will be the special badge of the professed children of God. Christians will love their own denominations less than they love the spirit and temper of the Christian, wherever it may be found.[11]

What does this mean? *Agreeing with everyone?* No. *Liking everyone's style or approach to Christianity?* No. It simply looks like choosing love over every bit of theology, preference or practice. It's having the wisdom to know that a family can have brothers and sisters who hold different points of view,

---

11   Barnes' Notes

but are bound together in love.

The Bible's most famous analogy of the church is like a human body with many parts. Paul describes the obvious logic behind being one body with many parts in 1 Corinthians 12. I'm sure that most Christians would agree with Paul's wisdom on the matter.

Yet, in practice, the most obvious teaching here is regularly disregarded or forgotten. It's almost as if there's an old sinful reflex in us – an unbroken habit of unredeemed life that leans into selfishness, pride and arrogance when it comes to what we believe – that rebels over and over again against the command to love.

That's why we need to be proactive and fight for unity. We need to discern that division is one of Satan's primary strategies to make God's people ineffective. We need to perceive that division costs us and robs us of the riches that comes with diversity, and all this needs to bother us enough to do something about it.

2
of the word

What do you think when you come across a church that advertises themselves as a 'Word-based' church? Do you sigh in relief because you know where you stand? Or, are you suspicious that they could be conservative or legalistic? What does this label mean anyway?

In the vast majority of my Christian life I've been a member of the same church, who I still see as my family. I never actually 'shopped' around for a church back then. I became a Christian through my sister's friendship group and I just inherited their church. It was relatively simple—it wasn't until I moved to America that we had to start looking. (A complicated process.) When you 'shop', you notice how churches advertise themselves. I've come across many church websites now that emphasize that they are indeed churches who are firmly founded and rooted in the Word.

For many who would label themselves as 'people of the Word', what they actually mean is that they are people of the Bible.

Most Christians would say that the Bible is important to them, but there are vast differences in how people interpret the Bible and varying levels of importance that people place on scripture. For those who label themselves as 'people of the

Word', what they are actually saying is that the Bible is the most important aspect of their faith.

For me, I have no problem at all with people who make this statement, how important the Bible is to each Christian is a choice I respect. What I'm concerned with, however, is the limited scope of what it means to be a 'Word" person. It's a label that Bible-passionate people have held onto, but one that I believe has much more depth to it than being 'people of scripture' alone.

The way I interpret being a person of the Word is *being a person who celebrates and treasures God's revelation to us.* This involves scripture, but also includes Jesus - the Word made flesh and prophecy - the present revelation from God.

The Word is simply how God communicates His love, His ways and His purpose for us. He does this throughout scripture and in His continuing communication to us through the gift of prophecy. The life of Jesus models it.

In scripture there are two different Greek words used for God's Word; *Logos* [12] and *Rhema* [13]. Logos refers to what's written, and Rhema refers to what's spoken. They are both ways that God has communicated His revelation to us through scripture (Logos) and through His continuing utterance (Rhema) via the Holy Spirit. Of course, the most profound revelation of God came through the life of Jesus—

---

12 Strong's Concordance #94487, Thomas Nelson Expanded Edition, April 11 2010
13 Strong's Concordance #93056, Thomas Nelson Expanded Edition, April 11 2010

scripture calls this *the Word made flesh*. Jesus came to represent God Himself.

> *The Son is the image of the invisible God, the firstborn over all creation.*[14]

> *The Son is the radiance of God's glory and the exact representation of his being, sustaining all things by his powerful word. After he had provided purification for sins, he sat down at the right hand of the Majesty in heaven*[15]

Because of this every born again believer of Jesus is a 'Word person'. The question, then, isn't whether we are Word people for the Christian this is like asking whether or not we are human. The real question is whether we embrace and value the *whole scope* of God's Word. Do we just focus on Jesus and ignore scripture and prophecy? Do we celebrate scripture but despise prophecy? Do we cherish the prophetic but handle scripture loosely?

I believe that we should celebrate, value and protect all of these aspects of God's Word.

The reason I'm writing this is not to ruffle the feathers of Bible-passionate Christians by stealing their label and redefining it. Rather, I'm so passionate about the Word I want everyone to understand what it involves, and how beneficial it can be in our lives.

---

14   Colossians 1:15 NIV
15   Hebrews 1:3 NIV

Let me share with you why I think the Word is so important to our Christian journey.

The Parable of the Sower

One of the most influential passages for me about God's Word is the parable of the sower found in three of the FOUR gospels. In this parable Jesus gives us some incredible truths about the Word of God:

> *While a large crowd was gathering and people were coming to Jesus from town after town, he told this parable: "A farmer went out to sow his seed. As he was scattering the seed, some fell along the path; it was trampled on, and the birds ate it up. Some fell on rocky ground, and when it came up, the plants withered because they had no moisture. Other seed fell among thorns, which grew up with it and choked the plants. Still other seed fell on good soil. It came up and yielded a crop, a hundred times more than was sown."*
>
> *When he said this, he called out, "Whoever has ears to hear, let them hear."* [16]

Jesus' parables can leave the reader full of questions. *What does this mean?* But in this parable Jesus gives a clear interpretation:

> *His disciples asked him what this parable meant. He said, "The knowledge of the secrets of the kingdom of God has been*

---

[16] Luke 8: 4-8 NIV

given to you, but to others I speak in parables, so that,

"'though seeing, they may not see; though hearing, they may not understand.'

"This is the meaning of the parable: The seed is the word of God. Those along the path are the ones who hear, and then the devil comes and takes away the word from their hearts, so that they may not believe and be saved. Those on the rocky ground are the ones who receive the word with joy when they hear it, but they have no root. They believe for a while, but in the time of testing they fall away. The seed that fell among thorns stands for those who hear, but as they go on their way they are choked by life's worries, riches and pleasures, and they do not mature. But the seed on good soil stands for those with a noble and good heart, who hear the word, retain it, and by persevering produce a crop.[17]

If this parable was made into a movie, the main **character** would be the seed of God's Word. The main **plot** would be *Does the seed get to fulfill it's destiny?* The **action** would involve the three villains (types of soil) that try and stop the seed reaching it's destiny (growing into maturity). Finally, the **hero** would be the good soil that figures out how to help the seed fulfill its purpose.

The Word of God is like a seed...

A seed.

---

17   Luke 8:9-15 NIV

Why would Jesus use this analogy for God's Word? This seed is the main character—but what is the significance of Jesus likening God's Word to a seed? There are a number of important attributes to a seed that have powerful implications when likened to God's Word:

Firstly, seeds are ALIVE. If you've ever opened a packet of seeds and poured them out on your hand the last thing you'll probably think is that these little hard, dry seeds are living. They don't move. They don't seem to do anything. But any botanist will tell you that seeds are in fact alive. Seeds use small amounts of stored energy to stay alive. They are waiting for the right conditions to grow.

Jesus wants us to know the nature of God's Word and that nature is that it's living! When you read scripture, or accept Jesus into your life, or receive a prophetic word, a seed is being planted within you—a tiny source of life that's waiting to grow.

Secondly, seeds have a PURPOSE. That purpose is to grow and bring more life. Even though seeds are alive, they are meant to be planted, grow and multiply. There is nothing static about God's Word. The Bible is alive, Jesus is alive, the prophetic word is living, and it doesn't stop there. God's Word has a dynamic purpose to re-create.

I remember talking with God while studying this passage one day. I was asking Him *"What does maturity look like?"* and *"If I'm meant to steward God's Word over my life or over a church or even a nation how do I know when I've done my job? What does it look like when it works? What does it look like when the*

Word has reached maturity?" I wasn't expecting an answer but I got one that shot through me like a lightning bolt. I heard the Holy Spirit's loud inner-voice tell me *"It's when the Word becomes flesh."*

After being stunned for a few minutes, God began unpacking what He meant. He was showing me that the His Word is successful *when we become the Word.*

It's when we become *what we read* in scripture, or when we become *like Jesus,* or when we become *the prophetic word* that's spoken over us.

Eat this Script

So when we read passages like the infamous 1 Corinthians 13 passage on love...

> *Love is patient and kind; love does not envy or boast; it is not arrogant or rude. It does not insist on its own way; it is not irritable or resentful; it does not rejoice at wrongdoing, but rejoices with the truth. Love bears all things, believes all things, hopes all things, endures all things.*

...what happens is a little seed is planted within us—a tiny piece of living treasure whose will is to re-create. For some who don't understand the Word's power or purpose, these passages can remain heartwarming niceties that become Christian ornaments adorning our spiritual wall. But for those who truly appreciate what this Word is meant to do—the people who wrestle with it, meditate on it, consume it—for those people, they find that this Word begins to re-create within them. They find a change takes place – selfish conditional love that has once ruled them is replaced by this beautiful depiction of what God's love looks like – this Word *becomes* them. The Word is made flesh.

Reproducing the Life of Jesus

Every Christian is to become a little Christ. The whole purpose of becoming a Christian is simply nothing else.[18]

There is no better example of God's word than Jesus. He is the Word that was made flesh. God's heart to communicate His love and His passion for us was so overwhelmingly huge that He sent His son to reveal the love of the Father.

And when we accept Him – His forgiveness, His salvation and His life – we accept the Word, and the Word is planted within us.

When we become a Christian, the whole point of our journey from here on out is to become like Christ. This miracle of salvation and re-birth into God's family allows us to grow into the family likeness. Once again the Word (Jesus) becomes flesh (is reproduced in our lives).

18 C.S. Lewis, Mere Christianity

Prophetic Flattery?

There are so many opinions on prophecy. The extremes range from *those who don't believe it's real* to those who take it to the extreme by overplaying how God speaks through every detail of life. As a pastor who teaches on the prophetic, I try to get real with this wonderful gift from the Holy Spirit. I would wholeheartedly and lovingly challenge any believer that buys into the belief that God doesn't speak today. How can we have a relationship with God our Father without dialogue? However, I also believe there's a lot to learn about *discerning* the prophetic word. Why? Because the authentic, prophetic word of God has the power to change lives.

God's prophetic word is like a powerful little seed budding with creative life. When God speaks over your life, the seed (Word) is longing to become flesh (transform you).

Prophetic words like

> *"You're called to be a prayer warrior"*

> *"God's put justice on your heart"*

> *"The father has a position for you in politics"*

Have become flesh (reached their purpose) when

> *"You are praying everyday and are leading others by example in prayer"*

"You are petitioning for justice"

"You are a politician or policy maker"

Every prophetic word has a dynamic power and purpose—it isn't God just making us feel good (although He does like to do that too). When God speaks, He speaks life. He speaks creation. He speaks destiny.

I hope you're getting the picture. God's word, scripture, the life of Jesus and the prophetic represent a dynamic force of life-giving power that's bursting to transform us from the inside out.

The Battle over the Word

The parable of the sower not only depicts the nature & purpose of God's Word, but it also shows us the very *present* reality that there is an overtly offensive effort to steal, rob and destroy the Word of God in our lives.

This should make us sit up and take notice. If there's that much energy (3 different types of soil) going into stopping the Word of God's purpose in our lives then it's because the Word is hugely profitable to us.

It seems like many Christians don't know how valuable the Word of God is for them. In Britain we have a TV program called *The Antiques Roadshow*. It's been running since I was a kid and I always remember watching it on Sunday afternoons. The gist of it is that the hopeful public can come into some big old venue with their household items and get them examined by antique experts. The best bit of the show for me was seeing the shocked face of the person who was told that the piece of china that they'd been using as a dog's feeding bowl 'all these years' was actually worth a fortune.

This program would always leave me with the haunting inner question of *do I have unknown treasures in my house?* What was insightful to me though was how different a piece would be treated once it was highly valued. When people realized the value of what they had in their possession, they would insure it and stop using it as a dog bowl, for example.

Until Christians understand the value of God's Word they probably won't treat it very well. They most likely won't be aware that the Word of God for their lives is one of the most valuable items on Satan's hit-list.

This parable shouts loudly to the hearer;

You have been given the most wonderful treasure—the Word of God. It's alive. It's ready to bring you *new life* to the level you cannot fathom. **But beware;** there are evil forces that will try their darnedest to steal this treasure from you.

The parable talks of three things that will attempt to take the seed away:

1. **The Path** is The Devil

2. **The Rock** is a time of testing

3. The Thorns are life's distractions

We need to be aware that the enemy doesn't want the Word of God to take root in our lives. He cannot do anything to separate us from the love of Christ, but he will try his best to make sure we're not fruitful. We need to be aware that when we receive a Word of revelation from God, there will be things around every corner trying to take that seed away.

Think about it. *Why are there so many false starts in our journey?*

Those moments where we're full of passion. Those times where we would lay our very lives down for Him. Those seasons where we believe that we are important in God's plan.

What happened? How did we forget? Did something distract us? How did life get so busy? How many seeds have been lost, stolen, and choked?

I've thought about it. When I've scanned through my history, in retrospect, I have seen all three types of conditions rear their ugly head soon after God's revelation comes. Whether it's been scripture, trying to be more like Jesus or a prophetic word that's been shared. Sometimes it's been subtle and other times it's been obvious.

Nowadays I can see it coming. For example, God starts stirring my heart about a passage of scripture. It might be out of a routine reading, but for some reason right now, this particular passage is stirring my heart. I start wrestling with it in my spirit. I start thinking *what does this mean for my life now?* And then, sure enough, something happens. The kids will get sick, for example. A week of sleepless nights and grumpy children goes by, and before I know it, that scripture is distant memory. The seed didn't get a chance to take root. It was snatched by the thorns in the parable.

We would do well to realize that – as we receive God's Word – there will more than likely be an effort to steal the seed. It might be that we get spiritually attacked or go through some hard times or simply get distracted. But through all of these times – if we're aware of what's happening – we will be prepared to hang on to the seed; the Word of life that's been given to us.

※

What does it mean to be a person of the Word? Well, it starts with Jesus. Becoming a Christian is accepting the Word into your life. From there it involves understanding the spectrum of God's communication to us that stretches from scripture to the Holy Spirit bringing His spoken word to us now. To grow as a person of the Word, it's crucial that we gain an understanding of the Word's value in our lives that will fuel us to not only celebrate it, but protect it and grow it.

3
of the spirit

As a prophetic pastor I've spent a lot of time teaching on how the Holy Spirit and His gifts are part of 'normal' Christianity. In those teachings I've had to untangle the confusion that some public expressions of the Spirit's gifts have left some Christians. I've had countless conversations with people who love God, but for one reason or another seem to think that the Spirit is assigned to a few very charismatic denominations. I find it difficult to reconcile this with my own experience, in which I see the Holy Spirit moving all over the place.

I believe wholeheartedly that the Holy Spirit is working in all denominations of churches. He's intimately close to all sorts of Christians with their differing aspects of theology and unique personalities. I see His breath of life weaving in and out of communities and the whispers that come with His faithful companionship are given to people of all nations.

He the Holy Spirit cannot and will not be contained in either a denomination or expression. God does not fit into our box.

It always saddens me when I meet people who are simply missing out on the Holy Spirit because of fears or misunderstandings, like Jane:

I met Jane in a Christian women's group. I had just moved to Huntington Beach, California and I needed to make new friends, so I joined this church group. In the first few meetings we started to get to know each other, shared about our families, our passions, what we did with our time. When I shared how I had been a pastor of a church, it immediately got their attention. Female pastors in American churches are still few and far between (although thankfully that's slowly changing). "So what did you do? Were you the women's pastor?" Jane asked, genuinely intrigued. "No, I was part of a team of pastors and I mainly taught people on the gifts of the Holy Spirit." I answered. "Oh so you went to a pentecostal church." Jane replied.

I sighed. *Really!? Since when did the mention of the Holy Spirit put me in a church denomination?* I was angry, not at Jane but at a culture that – for whatever reason – was boxing in the Holy Spirit and thus limiting people's exposure to Him. He is the gift Jesus so passionately told His disciples about:

> *If you love me, keep my commands. And I will ask the Father, and he will give you another advocate to help you and be with you forever–the Spirit of truth. The world cannot accept him, because it neither sees him nor knows him. But you know him, for he lives with you and will be in you.*[19]

How did we get to a place where good God-fearing people like Jane are saying things like this? How did we get to

---

19 John 14:15-17 NIV

a point where it's okay to disassociate ourselves with the Holy Spirit Himself for fear of being labeled with a certain denomination? I've met more people like Jane, who simply do not think that the Holy Spirit or His gifts are a major part of their journey. He is something they don't understand and the expressions they've seen (from afar) of Him are weird and slightly embarrassing.

What I hope to bring forth in this chapter is an understanding of the ways the Holy Spirit interacts with us in our everyday lives. It's this Holy companionship that really is the foundation of what it means to be a person of the Spirit. But before we unpack that, let's talk about the elephant in the room.

The extreme expressions of the Holy Spirit are what seem to cause the most angst or the most passion (depending upon which side of the fence one sits). These extreme expressions are long overdue for some wisdom and understanding. We need to know how to hold these appropriately in the context of our journey of faith.

Biblical Christianity is Full of the Weird, the Wacky and the Mysterious

It always baffles me when people who label themselves as 'people of the Word' have a problem with anything that's mysterious or supernatural. It just seems ironic as the Word that they defend is full of supernatural moments. Jesus being raised from the grave is a good one to start with. For the 'logically' minded Christian who steers clear of anything supernatural, I wonder how they have forgotten the fact that the central part of their faith is a crazy cataclysmic event that takes a huge step of faith to believe in. Not only that, but we have Jesus doing all sorts of 'supernatural' things under the anointing of the Holy Spirit; water into wine[20], walking on water[21], raising the dead[22], healing the sick[23] or multiplying food[24], to name a few.

I remember the first time I ever really considered that supernatural healing was part of today's Christian experience. I was a young Christian at the time. One Sunday as I sat in church, the pastor was interviewing a girl that had just come back from a mission trip in India. She was sharing stories of how people were getting healed—healed of some significant illnesses (not just the sniffles). She spoke of deformed hands straightening, the deaf hearing and the blind receiving sight. I sat there feeling bothered.

For some reason I found it hard to believe her, and this disbelief unsettled me. *Why did I find this hard to believe? How could I have faith to believe that supernatural events happened all those years ago in scripture and yet struggle to believe that God was active today?* I realized that I'd sanitized scripture. I'd heard those stories of Jesus so often that that's what they had become—nice Sunday school stories that had lost their punch. It was at that time in my life when I asked the Holy Spirit to help me re-read the Bible with fresh eyes. I asked Him to

---

20 John 2:1-11
21 Matthew 14:22-33
22 Luke 7:11-17
23 Mark 1:34
24 Matthew 14:13-21

take away any over-familiarity that had grown and blurred my vision. After that, I was wowed when I read the gospels.

Fearing the Spiritual

It's important to know that it's okay to have a fear of the spiritual. It's normal to fear the unexplainable or supernatural. When you look at the stories in scripture of people encountering this type of phenomena, usually their first response is fear:

The Angel Gabriel told Mary not to be afraid as he told her of her virgin birth:

> *The angel went to her and said, "Greetings, you who are highly favored! The Lord is with you." Mary was greatly troubled at his words and wondered what kind of greeting this might be. But the angel said to her, "Do not be afraid, Mary; you have found favor with God. You will conceive and give birth to a son, and you are to call him Jesus."* [25]

John fainted in his revelatory experience:

> *I, John, your brother and companion in the suffering and kingdom and patient endurance that are ours in Jesus, was on the island of Patmos because of the word of God and the testimony of Jesus. On the Lord's Day I was in the Spirit, and I heard behind me a loud voice like a trumpet, which*

---

[25] Luke 1:28-31 NIV

said: "Write on a scroll what you see and send it to the seven churches: to Ephesus, Smyrna, Pergamum, Thyatira, Sardis, Philadelphia and Laodicea."

I turned around to see the voice that was speaking to me. And when I turned I saw seven golden lampstands, and among the lampstands was someone like a son of man, dressed in a robe reaching down to his feet and with a golden sash around his chest. The hair on his head was white like wool, as white as snow, and his eyes were like blazing fire. His feet were like bronze glowing in a furnace, and his voice was like the sound of rushing waters. In his right hand he held seven stars, and coming out of his mouth was a sharp, double-edged sword. His face was like the sun shining in all its brilliance.

When I saw him, I fell at his feet as though dead. Then he placed his right hand on me and said: "Do not be afraid. I am the First and the Last. I am the Living One; I was dead, and now look, I am alive for ever and ever! And I hold the keys of death and Hades.

"Write, therefore, what you have seen, what is now and what will take place later. The mystery of the seven stars that you saw in my right hand and of the seven golden lampstands is this: The seven stars are the angels of the seven churches, and the seven lampstands are the seven churches."[26]

Fear of the spiritual realm is a normal human response.

---

[26] Revelation 1:9-20 NIV

The Bible talks about it as awe.[27] The challenging aspect of this reaction, however, is when it grows and joins with our other fleshly fears and ultimately leads us into disbelief. When we encounter something spiritual we can be afraid—it's understandable since it's outside of our framework for reason. But we need to know that when we're presented with something like this in our lives, it's like a door that God places in front of us leading to a journey of a deeper understanding of His Kingdom. He wants us wrestle with it, to work out what we believe with fear and trembling.

So it's certainly fine to be hesitant – it's par for the course to question – but when we embrace disbelief, we shut the door. We say *this door doesn't even exist.* We block it out and we remove ourselves from the uncomfortable-but-fascinating journey into the knowledge of God's world, a world we will be part of forever.

Fear that leads to disbelief is certainly the core stumbling block preventing many people from embracing the Spirit in their lives. There are two major realities from the Christian world that fuel this fear and disbelief. These are realities that we need to take responsibility for and try to remedy.

1. Lack of Authenticity

First is the question of authenticity. Unfortunately, in the midst of some very real encounters and expressions of the Holy Spirit, there are exaggerated accounts and

27   Psalm 33:8

human-induced states. For some, this lack of authenticity keeps them miles away from anything spiritual. Usually, this matters more to characters that are highly principled and more black and white in their thinking. The response to the people struggling with this lack of authenticity by those regarding themselves as 'full of the Spirit' is one of frustration. Instead of respecting the fact that some personalities process things differently, some 'Spirit-filled' people brand them as 'religious' or 'legalistic'—further widening the divide and fueling misunderstanding.

There are two main areas where authenticity can seem questionable:

a) Testimony - a Story of what God has Done

This could be supernatural healing, a miracle, a visitation of an angel or some other unusual spiritual experience. Sometimes, as we communicate these experiences, we tend to exaggerate them or even add to them. At times we share based on some second hand information that simply hasn't been accurate or has accumulated into a spiritual version of Chinese whispers.

The consequences of this sloppy type of communication has been one of the hardest lessons I've learned as a minister. Being too eager or too emotional about a testimony has created stumbling blocks for others around me. This is such a sad reality for someone like me who longs to encourage people in their journey of faith.

For quite some time this used to frustrate me. *Surely mistakes can happen right? Why do people get so worked up if a healing story that's told actually pans out slightly differently? Do they not know my heart? Do they think I would knowingly share wrong information?* For many years I thought this was other people's problem for not being more gracious. But I've come to learn that actually this is my responsibility. A testimony of Jesus is such a precious thing, it has power to change lives and we should handle it with care.

Not only do we need to be rigorous in the accuracy in our telling of stories, we need to be as inclusive as possible. One of my practices as a prophetic pastor was to try to de-mystify spiritual language. It was a standard I held for myself and one I asked of those that I taught and discipled. There are so many spiritual sayings that have accumulated in our Christian culture. A lot of people don't understand these 'in' sayings and often feel left out.

"God spoke to me this morning..."

For the new Christian or someone who hasn't been exposed to any prophetic teaching, this saying can be taken literally. Translated to novice ears *"God audibly spoke to me"*. Broad statements like this can make others feel disqualified, as they might not have heard God 'audibly' speak to them, the conclusion they draw is that they are not very spiritual. I used to press the point to my prophetic team:

How did God speak to you? What language did He use? Because that statement could be read a thousand ways;

"I was reading the bible this morning and I felt God speak to me as a verse just stood out."

"I was taking a walk this morning and as I looked at the beautiful creation I felt God stir some thoughts."

"I awoke this morning with a vivid dream imprinted in my mind – I felt that God was highlighting things."

"When I was drinking my coffee this morning I had a strange picture in my mind which I felt was from God."

"As I was taking a shower this morning I was rather shocked but for the first time I heard the audible voice of God."

The result of this discipline is that the more details are shared, the more people can identify. Identification with a testimony makes people feel included, like they are part of it, that it can happen to them—this is essential in empowering everyone to hear from God for themselves. The same is true for recounting stories of the miraculous or spiritual. Being as clear and accurate as possible without sensationalism is the key to blessing the most amount of people with a God testimony. Authentic God stories don't need any extras, they stand tall and glorious as monuments of His goodness and glory.

b) Physical Reactions to the Holy Spirit

Shaking, laughing, weeping, dancing, falling over in a Spirit induced drunkenness. This is an issue of much controversy. There are those who believe these reactions are *emotionally induced, culturally learned* or even *demonic.*

Regarding this issue there are at least 4 different things we can believe:

1. Everyone who is reacting in a physical manner is 100% reacting to the Holy Spirit.

2. There is a mixture of stuff going on. Some of it's genuine, some emotional, some 'learned'.

3. None of it is authentic. We don't believe the Holy Spirit effects people this way.

4. These reactions are demonic.

I like option 2; that there's a mixture of stuff going on. I do believe that people's bodies can react when the Holy Spirit is around (because I'm one of them). Some more than others. I don't, however, believe it's indicative of the state of a person's spiritual maturity or whether they are getting blessed by God. In my experience, different people are sensitive to different things, and react in different ways. This is why I'd rather call it a physical *reaction* to the Holy Spirit's presence rather than a *manifestation of the Spirit* (which implies something happening outside of our control).

The manifestations of the Spirit that we see in the Bible weren't physical reactions to the Spirit, instead they were the gifts of the Spirit that would manifest themselves in a person, enabling that person to actively move forward in that gift.

> *Now to each one the manifestation of the Spirit is given for the common good. To one there is given through the Spirit a message of wisdom, to another a message of knowledge by means of the same Spirit, to another faith by the same Spirit, to another gifts of healing by that one Spirit, to*

another miraculous powers, to another prophecy, to another distinguishing between spirits, to another speaking in different kinds of tongues, and to still another the interpretation of tongues. All these are the work of one and the same Spirit, and he distributes them to each one, just as he determines.[28]

So why would some people react physically and others not when the Holy Spirit's presence is around? I believe this is mainly due to our sensitivity. We're all sensitive to different things, some individuals I believe are more sensitive with the connectivity of body, mind and spirit than others. We know that our body mind and spirit are interrelated. Physiological ailments like anxiety, fear and stress often manifest physically. If the body responds to the mind, how much more can it respond to the Spirit?

What's also interesting is that some people are affected more than others. For example, if I have been shocked by something, my body physically shakes for a few minutes but for my husband Chris his body would rarely react in this way.

Should it surprise us that some people's bodies shake or fall over when God's Spirit is present? And should it surprise us that some people's bodies react while others don't?

Whether this physical reaction is due to the Holy Spirit being present, or whether it's due to 'learned' behavior or sensationalism is the real question. Can it be the Holy Spirit?

---

28 1 Corinthians 12:7 -11 NIV

I believe yes, absolutely. Is it always the Holy Spirit? *No*, not always.

A further and perhaps more important question is *how much does this matter?* For the highly principled character it probably matters a lot—they only want the real deal and nothing more. However, I would like to pose another question. *How realistic is this?* In every other part of our lives, our expressions and reactions are a mixture of physical, emotional and spiritual. *Do we demand such rigorous separation of body, mind, spirit in same way we interpret the Bible?* No, indeed not. In fact, we celebrate the fact that our intellect plays a crucial role or our emotions come into play as we read books such as the Psalms.

Should it shock us that there may be 'learned' behavior in such reactions to the Holy Spirit, when that's exactly what culture itself is? All around our churches we have 'learned' behavior, our spiritual language is full of it. Do we get hung up on whether it's authentic, or do we just accept that it's part of human nature to copy and create patterns of behavior? Why then are we so shocked that – when people react physically to the Holy Spirit – that these human traits are mixed in with the experience?

For me, when I watch a group who are expressing physical reactions to the presence of God, I expect a certain amount of emotionalism and even a little 'learned' behavior. It doesn't bother me when I know that the heart of these people is to worship God. I guess the only time when this matters to me is when I see it taken to the extreme, when emotional sensationalism and 'learned' behavior take the dominant place, creating a need-driven environment rather than authentic worship.

So what's to be done with this issue of authenticity? While we certainly can't police this across the church, we *can* make decisions about our own approach. For those of you who find this lack of authenticity an obstacle in embracing the Spirit, it's important you gain some understanding as to why this happens. Is it really the devil or is it more just the flaws of humanity? Can you find in your heart some grace for this? For those of you who experience the Spirit *physically* and are frustrated by those that question it's authenticity, it might be a good idea to understand that striving for authenticity will help bridge the gap.

2. Limited Focus on the Extreme

The other area that can fuel disbelief of the spiritual is the way we've limited our focus on these extreme expressions. The message received by some is that *to be a person of the Holy Spirit means you need to shake in worship or fall over on the floor.* While these physical reactions do happen, I believe we are doing the Holy Spirit a huge disservice by suggesting that this is all He does. We need teaching and good practice where we show all of the ways the Holy Spirit can affect our lives. It's not that the extreme isn't important. It is. But there needs to be more chapters written, more stories told that widen the playing field on how great and wonderful it is for us to have the Holy Spirit with us here on Earth.

Friendship with the Holy Spirit

A few years ago I remember having a conversation with my husband Chris about his work. Chris is a designer, writer and entrepreneur. We were in the kitchen talking about some of his frustrations regarding design work. Through the conversation we hit a bit of revelation. Jokingly I asked him, *if there was a hero of his in his field that he could spend a couple of hours with, picking their brain, who would it be?* Immediately he said Jony Ive[29] and expanded by saying how awesome that would be. I said *Well you know that God's a better designer than Jonathan Ive and you can spend as much time as you want with Him.* For both of us in that moment, we 'grasped' a bit of knowledge—the wonder of what was at our fingertips because of the gift of the Holy Spirit. Chris could dream with God, tap into His expertise, wisdom and creativity because His Spirit is living in us.

There are many roles that the Holy Spirit can play in our lives; helper, counselor, teacher, comforter. If you've been part of a church for any length of time, you might have received some teaching on this. The roles, gifts, fruits, descriptions of the Holy Spirit in scripture are all good to learn. But I wonder sometimes if, by focusing on these things alone, we subtly lose the glorious truth of who He is and what this means for us. He can too easily become a commodity.

We need to begin by understanding how integral the Holy Spirit is to our journey of faith. How He rebirths us into

---

29 designer at Apple

God's Kingdom as joint heirs with Jesus and how He then indwells in us as we live out our days so that we can access intimacy with God. This is an outstanding revelation. And when one grasps it, the debate as to *whether we are people of the Spirit or not* becomes as ridiculous as questioning whether human beings have blood in their bodies.

I believe there's been a huge lack of teaching on the role of the Holy Spirit in that miraculous moment of when a person becomes a Christian. And it's due to this sloppy 'let's get them saved, it's as easy as A-B-C' approach that we now have many Christians who don't properly understand the Holy Spirit, and actually fear Him instead of understanding that He is there to be the very best friend in a Christian's life. This is largely down to the fact that we find it hard to talk about mystery. We'd rather reduce things down and ignore the mysterious than grapple with it.

The reality is that the whole Trinity is at work in the born again experience;

The Father has the desire for all people to be reconciled to Him. He is the visionary.

Jesus makes it possible. By becoming the 'lamb' that was slain, He pays the debt of sin making it possible for every person enter the Kingdom of God. He is the conqueror.

> *he saved us, not because of righteous things we had done, but because of his mercy. He saved us through the washing of*

rebirth and renewal by the Holy Spirit[30]

The Holy Spirit rebirths us—makes us new spiritual beings that belong to the family of God. He also indwells in us bringing rehabilitation, healing and understanding about our new identity as sons and daughters of God. He is the enabler.

The truth is that we can't become a born again Christian without the Holy Spirit, just like we can't become a Christian without the cross. The Father's vision was to have His sons and daughters back. In order to do this Jesus needed to free us from the slavery of sin by laying His life down as the ultimate sacrifice. The Holy Spirit hovered over the grave and brought resurrection life to Jesus first, and then to anyone who believes in Jesus. It's the Spirit who rebirths us into God's family.

I love that it doesn't stop there. We could have been saved (by Jesus) and reborn (by the Holy Spirit) and then left to wait until we die or Jesus returns to develop our relationship with the Father to spend time with our spiritual Dad. But no—that wasn't good enough for the Father (who Jesus depicts in the story of the prodigal son as one that's pacing up and down looking out for His lost children). The Father wants intimacy *now*. That's why the Holy Spirit is a gift to us. When He indwells in us we are connected to the Father and we're able to gain friendship with God.

It's truly remarkable that each one of us is able to have a friendship with God, something that was unattainable before

---

30 Titus 3:5 NIV

the cross due to the divide of sin. It's this intimacy with God that is the overarching banner of all good things. For Chris, at times, it means having God to fuel his creativity. For some it's having God's counsel in a time of change, and for others it's a comforter in times of grief. Like all friends that play different roles across the span of a lifetime, the Holy Spirit interweaves throughout the seasons of our lives. He becomes many different things to us according to our need. He is our great partner and He is our friend.

Being a person of the Spirit really begins when a person becomes a Christian. We become a person of the Spirit when we are reborn by Him into God's family. This is the foundation that the Holy Spirit lays. A new identity and a new intimacy. From this foundation many things of the Spirit can grow but unless we fully grasp this footing we can be easily waylaid.

Baptism of the Holy Spirit

Historically, Pentecost followed Calvary; experientially, being filled with the power of the Holy Spirit follows the bearing of the cross.[31]

As Christians we are naturally people of the Spirit because it's He who rebirths us and gives us our membership into the body of Christ. Our conversion experience is all about our identity—the cross allows us to be adopted into the family

---

31 Watchman Nee, Journeying towards the spiritual: A digest of the spiritual man in 42 lessons - lesson 17, p88)

of God.

But from that place comes a call to join the cause of Christ. It's primarily a call to save the world; to be Christ's representatives on Earth that carry His mandate. Nothing sums up Christ's cause better than Isaiah 61, in which Jesus himself declared of Himself in the temple. It's the job description of a savior:

> *The Spirit of God, the Master, is on me because God anointed me. He sent me to preach good news to the poor, heal the heartbroken, Announce freedom to all captives, pardon all prisoners. God sent me to announce the year of his grace—a celebration of God's destruction of our enemies— and to comfort all who mourn, To care for the needs of all who mourn in Zion, give them bouquets of roses instead of ashes,*
>
> *Messages of joy instead of news of doom, a praising heart instead of a languid spirit. Rename them "Oaks of Righteousness" planted by God to display his glory.*[32]

How each one of us carries this out will be uniquely crafted according to our gifts and context. But the call, in essence, is the same.

So what does the baptism of the Spirit have to do with all this? I know that for some of us there's confusion about what this means, when it happens and what it's for.

---

32 Isaiah 61:1-7 The Message

Biblically, we see that Jesus is considered to be the first one baptized by the Spirit, and it happens at the same time of His water baptism with John. The Spirit comes upon Jesus as a dove and rests on him. According to scripture, the Spirit empowers Jesus and this baptism is a marker of His initiation into ministry. It's John the Baptist who first coined this phrase "baptized by the Holy Spirit"; he points to Jesus and says of Him that 'He will baptize with the Holy Spirit and fire."

Later on in the book of Acts we see further references to this baptism of the Spirit. Jesus Himself prepares His disciples for their baptism of the Spirit:

> *And being assembled together with them, He commanded them not to depart from Jerusalem, but to wait for the Promise of the Father, "which," He said, "you have heard from Me; for John truly baptized with water, but you shall be baptized with the Holy Spirit not many days from now."* [33]

The disciples received their dramatic baptism of the Spirit at Pentecost:

> *When the day of Pentecost arrived, they were all together in one place. And suddenly there came from heaven a sound like a mighty rushing wind, and it filled the entire house where they were sitting. And divided tongues as of fire appeared to them and rested on each one of them. And they were all filled with the Holy Spirit and began to speak in*

---

[33] Acts 1:4-5 NKJV

other tongues as the Spirit gave them utterance.[34]

While Jesus was preparing the disciples for this baptism of the Spirit, He talked about them being "clothed with power from on high." Again, it was about being *empowered for ministry* that seemed to be the key reason for this mysterious wild act of the Spirit. From Pentecost we see the disciples powerfully gifted and fully entering their ministries.

So what does the baptism of the Spirit mean for us, and when does it occur? There are diverse opinions on this ranging from different Christian traditions. But they can mainly be put into 3 categories:

1. The Baptism of the Spirit comes specifically to join us into the family of God. People who take this theological stance believe that the Spirit's baptism happens either upon conversion or around one's baptism of water.

2. The Baptism of the Spirit comes to bestow people with Spiritual gifts. Jesus and His disciples went on to perform miracles, healing and deliverance directly after their baptism of the Spirit. The disciples also began speaking in a heavenly language (The gift of tongues).

3. The Baptism of the Spirit comes to bring empowerment for Christian ministry.

Many Christians firmly reside in one of these theological

---

[34] Acts 2:1-4 ESV

camps. I've never really been one of those people. I've decided to live with a certain level of mystery on this spiritual act. This isn't because I don't think it's important, it's because I believe the Holy Spirit's acts can't be pinned down to human explanation entirely. My journey, my understanding of scripture and who I know the Holy Spirit to be leads me to believe that the Holy Spirit baptizes us for all of the above reasons and His baptism or 'clothing us with power' happens more than once during a lifetime.

I also believe that there are a number of downfalls that happen when one begins to be too specific about why the baptism of the Spirit happens and when it should happen to a believer. Namely that believers start questioning their own experience, doubting whether or not they've had the full experience. When we compare ourselves and our spiritual experiences to others we can all too easily live with a sense of having 'missed out' rather than living with the security of abundance. And the Bible tells us that God gives us the Spirit without measure!

> *For He whom God has sent speaks the words of God, for God does not give the Spirit by measure.*[35]

If I looked at the disciples' experience at Pentecost and at other testimonies of people's extraordinary encounters with the Spirit as the only standard of baptism of the Spirit, then I would probably feel quite unworthy. Now I choose to trust who I know the Holy Spirit to be. He's my ever faithful companion; the one who leads me into all truth. He's so

---

35 John 3:34 NKJV

passionate about me being everything I'm created to be that I have no doubt He has initiated His anointing bringing adoption, empowerment and gifts in the correct seasons of my life. Some of them have been dramatic, others more subtle.

Instead of getting caught up in the technicalities of baptism of the Spirit, I try and cultivate a heart to receive it, to understand why this 'pouring out' or 'clothing' of His power is so vital for me. I try and make a practice of looking back over the course of my life to see His distinct wisdom, recognizing when and where He's clothed me anew with spiritual gifts, a compassionate heart, boldness, vision and a desire for God's kingdom.

And when I do look back I see a delicate path that only He could have laid out before me; an interweaving of the Holy Spirit through my life that distinctly knows when to bring gifts, when to bring power and when to bring a deepening of my identity as a daughter of God.

If you're someone that's been put off or put down by others' definitions of the Spirit's baptism, I'd like to encourage you to see it for what it really is in it's simplest form—an investment from the Spirit into you to become all that you're meant to be. The Spirit's passion for this cause far outweighs any restrictions we can put on Him.

I believe that, deep down, there's a resonance with Christ's cause in all of us. People of all ages, races and religions want to save the world in some way, shape or form. Sometimes this pure resemblance of our creator is distorted in some way by the systems of this world or our experience with sin. But original goodness exists in each and every person.

As a child I had a recurring dream for a couple years; I'd be a superhero with my two best friends Rachel and Lesley. We'd be playing together, but then some kind of crisis would present itself and we would grab our superhero capes and fly off to save the day. I would always wear a blue cape, Rachel wore red and Lesley's was yellow.

Looking back I think it must have been to do with a little too much TV and maybe a deep core desire to be someone who could help save the world. (Deep stuff for an 8 year old.)

For those of us who are reborn into the family of God, the Spirit longs to breathe on this original light within us. He wants to kindle this desire to save the world with Jesus into a wildfire that cannot be contained. This is why He baptizes us.

Walking with the Spirit

If we live in the Spirit, let us also walk in the Spirit.[36]

Our family now lives in the foothills of the Rocky Mountains; in Fort Collins, Colorado. Our favorite activity is to make use of the many beautiful hiking trails on our doorstep. We take the kids walking each week to teach them about nature and to get the whole family outside.

---

36 Galatians 5:25 KJV

On any given walk there are several dynamics that take place when we walk together. I recently returned from a 4-mile hike with the kids where we taught them a number of things; we needed to enforce that they stayed close (as we were near a place where coyotes frequent). Then, as we climbed a bit, we had to hold their hands to make sure they didn't fall over the rocks.

When I picture what *walking with the Holy Spirit* looks like, I can see all sorts of similar dynamics happening; those times where it feels like the Holy Spirit has been holding my hand, and seasons where He's told me to stay close.

Walking with the Spirit mirrors the many seasons of life we go through, and the many different roles He plays as our great friend and companion. But walking with the Spirit is also more than that.

The Apostle Paul suggested in his letter to the church in Galatia that there was a difference between living with the Spirit and walking with the Spirit.

My love for walking started while living in Bristol, UK. Every day I would walk the hilly streets – taking me from one meeting to another – sometimes covering more than 5 miles a day. This built up my stamina to be a very fast and efficient walker.

One time I was away in Frankfurt for a weekend with Church Missions Society. Through a series of meetings, we were exploring what emerging church could look like. After one late meeting finishing around 10pm, we left as a group to walk back to our hotel. Due to my ability to walk very fast I was at the front of the pack chatting in depth with a friend and colleague. I hadn't realized that the rest of the group thought I was leading the way back to the hotel (which was the farthest thing from my mind). I assumed someone else knew where they were going and this led to a two hour ramble around Frankfurt in the middle of the night.

Lots of lessons were learned that night. (Mainly that I had no sense of direction whatsoever.)

When Paul talks about the difference of *living* with the Spirit and *walking* with the Spirit, I believe the hinge-pin lies in *who's leading the way. Is it you or is it Him? Who's in charge?* It's one thing to enjoy the fact that the Holy Spirit is present with us, it's quite another to let Him lead you and bring direction to your journey.

Walking with the Spirit is choosing to *follow His lead* with the innate understanding that He's our best guide. It's relinquishing the right to be independent in our choices, and accepting that the fast way isn't always the right way.

I've met very few Christians who continually walk with the Spirit in this way; a way that truly follows The Spirit's lead. It's often something we dip in and out of depending on how successful our lives are going. I've found that, generally, when people are in crisis the desire to let Him lead becomes stronger.

Fully embracing a walk with the Spirit demands *letting go of our control*—which seems at-odds with human nature. And even for those who give themselves in full abandonment to the Spirit's direction, the pace of life itself upsets the nature of 'keeping in step' with Him.

But when we do choose to walk with Him, we can find ourselves on a wild ride where we question *why on Earth we don't do this all the time?* We end up having significant connections, unplanned adventures, and we come alive.

Risking Unplanned Routes

When Chris and I were first married we took a road trip through France with my sister and her family. We'd booked a French bed and breakfast (B&B) for one evening that was a couple of miles away from my sister's. We arrived at their B&B quite late at night. We dropped them off and were ready to find our own for the night. My brother-in-law had set up the GPS for us and we were ready to go. (These were old school days and we had a good old fashioned Garmin GPS.)

As we left – eager for our destination – we drove down a major road for 5 minutes when the GPS told us to *turn left*. The only problem was that *left* seemed to indicate that we drive through a forest. My husband's eyes lit up (he loves off-roading). I, however, was way more cautious. *We are in France, it's dark, and you want to take me through a forest!?* When you're used to a road it's hard to choose a forest. Everything within me thought this was a bad idea, but before I had a chance we were driving through thick trees on an old, unpaved road.

As my visions of us spending the night *stuck in a ditch*

somewhere while listening to the creatures of the night dissipated, I actually began to enjoy this unexpected route. It was weird and slightly thrilling. Sure enough, this route took us directly to our lovely 17th century quaint B&B that seemed to be in the middle of nowhere. We found out later that my brother-in-law had forgotten to turn off the *old unpaved roads* option on the GPS.

If you choose to walk with the Spirit, it won't be long before you find out that He has many old unpaved roads. His ways are not our ways. He will ask you to go in directions that might not make sense to our human reason—directions that may take you across unusual terrain. The key here is *will you trust Him?* Will you trust the voice that tells you to go through the forest in the middle of the night?

Taking the risk to trust Him is the beginning of truly walking with the Spirit. From there on in it's really about learning how to live our daily lives while tuned into His voice, making sure we acknowledge His ever present counsel with us. It's choosing to, moment by moment, ask Him what He thinks and seek His direction.

Being a person of the Spirit really has nothing to do with which denomination of church you belong to. It has nothing to do with what type of personality you are or what upbringing you've had. What it has everything to do with is our identity as reborn sons and daughters of God. As He rebirths us, He indwells in us so that we can have intimacy with the Father; friendship with the creator of the universe!

From there on out, the Holy Spirit becomes our biggest advocate. He empowers us, gives us spiritual gifts and walks with us, leading our journey. This is what it really means to be a person of the Spirit.

4
cornerstone

Therefore, this is what the Sovereign LORD says: "Look! I am placing a foundation stone in Jerusalem, a firm and tested stone. It is a precious cornerstone that is safe to build on. Whoever believes need never be shaken." [37]

A Vision of Jesus

When I was in my twenties I had one of the most profound dreams of my life. To this day it remains a treasure to me.

In the dream I was walking around a city. The environment felt chaotic. There was lots of hustle and bustle. I remember feeling cluttered in my thinking, that I had no real sense of peace, that I was somehow confused.

I looked up and saw a mountain in the distance on the outskirts of the city. I felt this irresistible need to go and climb this mountain.

As I reached the mountain, an old monastery came

---

[37] Isaiah 28:16 NLT

into view. It was right at the top. I began to climb. The monastery had an ancient door that was so heavy that opening it required all my weight. When I entered, streams of light flooded the building. Beauty seemed to live in every stone of every wall.

As I turned around I saw Jesus. He was up so close; his joy-filled face scanning mine. His gleaming eyes saw me. In that moment I felt fully loved and fully known—a feeling I'd never felt before or since. It was a feeling that is too hard to describe. He told me that He loved me and that He would be there with me through every day of my life and then through eternity.

This dream is the closest thing I've had to an 'encounter' dream; like the biblical account of the angel that visited Joseph in his dream. These types of dreams are a real encounter, but mysteriously hosted in a dream. Even though it was many years ago, I can instantly remember everything about it; the feelings, smells and sights. It's a dream that centers me. *Jesus. He is all I need. He is my foundation. My solid ground.*

There are many names for Jesus in the Bible but my favorite is *The Cornerstone*. The cornerstone, in building terms, is the first stone set. Every other stone follows it. It's also called the *foundation* stone. Jesus didn't come to construct a building, but this analogy speaks loudly of how His life, His teaching, His ways need to be the first stone set for our faith—the foundation. When we are grappling with what we believe, we must look to Him first.

When I think of my journey of faith I'm aware of how many things, people and churches have influenced my beliefs. This is normal to a certain degree—God's put us into a family of believers and uses others to shape and direct us. However, it's always really important to keep going back to the source of our faith: Jesus Himself.

Sometimes I wonder whether Jesus gets lost in the swath of other people's teaching, insights and wisdom. We're living in an era of unprecedented access to resources like podcasts, books and conferences. We have these available in unlimited supply and – while that is a blessing from God – we mustn't let these things *alone* shape our faith and beliefs.

When I'm in a reflective, self-challenging mood I ask myself these questions: *Where do I get my vision from? Why do I believe what I believe? Do my beliefs match up to the life of Jesus—what He taught and demonstrated?*

Quite often I'm shocked that I'm more influenced by second, third or fourth interpretations of a truth than going to the source Himself. Such can be the nature of Western Christianity.

This is why I wanted to write this chapter; I wanted to start by looking at the life of Jesus in the context of the Word and Spirit. It's simply no good me *flying this flag* if actually the Word and the Spirit was insignificant to Jesus.

Jesus - a Man of the Word and Spirit

There are many ways to approach this analysis of where the Word and Spirit fall within the life of Jesus. I could examine all of his teaching on the subject or look at all of the verses covering these topics, but I want to focus on some of the areas of His life where the Word and Spirit are inextricably linked. To me, this – more than anything – shows how these two should be held together in the life of a Christian. For *surely it's His example* that we're following.

Jesus' Birth

He was the Word made flesh who was conceived by the Holy Spirit.

The place to start is at Jesus' birth. It amazes me that right at the beginning of His life on Earth, as the very purposes of God were unraveling, we see the role of the Word and the activity of the Spirit. These are not just hot topics, these are part of Jesus' very being. His identity and purpose as the Son of Man who came to save the World was formed and initiated by the Word and the Spirit. He was the Word made flesh. He was conceived by the Holy Spirit in Mary who carried Him as a baby. This is once again an outstanding vision of the whole Trinity working together to see salvation realized for humankind.

The gospel of John explicitly talks about Jesus being *the Word who becomes flesh:*

> *In the beginning was the Word, and the Word was with God, and the Word was God. He was with God in the beginning. Through him all things were made; without him nothing was made that has been made. In him was life, and that life was the light of all mankind. The light shines in the darkness, and the darkness has not overcome it.*[38]

And then,

> *The Word became flesh and made his dwelling among us. We have seen his glory, the glory of the one and only Son, who came from the Father, full of grace and truth.*[39]

The life of Jesus is the greatest expression of God's Word, His message to us of who He is, how much He loves us and what hope there is in being part of His family. The law and the prophets came first to show in-part who God was, but they were incomplete, so God sent His son to be a full representation of the Father, so that all might see and know a God of love who offers salvation, intimacy and eternal life.

The book of Hebrews puts it like this:

> *The Son is the radiance of God's glory and the exact representation of his being, sustaining all things by his powerful word. After he had provided purification for sins, he sat down at the right hand of the Majesty in heaven.*[40]

---

38   John 1:1-5 NIV
39   John 1:14 NIV
40   Hebrews 1:3 NIV

Jesus is the Word made flesh:

Jesus *became* flesh by the Holy Spirit. The Bible tells us that it was the Holy Spirit that conceived Jesus as He overshadowed Mary. What a miracle! It's another one of those 'Sunday school' stories to which it's all too easy to nod our heads in agreement… but when you stop and think about it, it can blow your mind! Here's an account from Matthew:

> *This is how the birth of Jesus the Messiah came about: His mother Mary was pledged to be married to Joseph, but before they came together, she was found to be pregnant through the Holy Spirit. Because Joseph her husband was faithful to the law, and yet did not want to expose her to public disgrace, he had in mind to divorce her quietly.*
>
> *But after he had considered this, an angel of the Lord appeared to him in a dream and said, "Joseph son of David, do not be afraid to take Mary home as your wife, because what is conceived in her is from the Holy Spirit. She will give birth to a son, and you are to give him the name Jesus, because he will save his people from their sins."* [41]

The significance of this is that we're shown a great partnership of the Word & the Spirit as they initiate the Father's dream. Right at the beginning of the life of Jesus, these two walk hand in hand.

---

41   Matthew 1:18-21 NIV

Jesus' Baptism

Affirmed by the Word and Anointed by the Spirit

Jesus' Baptism was a major event in His life; it marked the beginning of His ministry and was a public demonstration of the partnership of the Word and Spirit endorsing His life.

The scene is set with the prophet John's ministry. John was described in the Bible as *a man who lived off locusts and wild honey, wearing clothes of camel's hair.*[42] He had a large following who were captivated by his teaching on baptism of repentance and forgiveness of sin.

One day as he is preaching, prophesying and baptizing, Jesus comes from Galilee and asks John to baptize Him. John humbly concedes, even though intuitively he knows Jesus is the Messiah.

> *Then Jesus came from Galilee to the Jordan to be baptized by John. But John tried to deter him, saying, "I need to be baptized by you, and do you come to me?"*
>
> *Jesus replied, "Let it be so now; it is proper for us to do this to fulfill all righteousness." Then John consented.*
>
> *As soon as Jesus was baptized, he went up out of the water. At that moment heaven was opened, and he saw the Spirit of God descending like a dove and alighting on him. And a*

---

42 Matthew 3:4

voice from heaven said, "This is my Son, whom I love; with him I am well pleased." [43]

And so we have this epic scene of an open heaven where the Word and Spirit are publicly affirming His life. The Word of the Father comes audibly to approve Jesus identity as God's son, boast His undeniable love for Him, and bring praise to His journey so far. In the same moment the Spirit descends like a dove and rests on Jesus.

This is all done with crowds watching, those present must have been blown away. Later the next day, John the Baptist attests to what happened and confirms to his followers that Jesus is the Messiah.

> *The next day John saw Jesus coming toward him and said, "Look, the Lamb of God, who takes away the sin of the world! This is the one I meant when I said, 'A man who comes after me has surpassed me because he was before me.' I myself did not know him, but the reason I came baptizing with water was that he might be revealed to Israel."*
>
> *Then John gave this testimony: "I saw the Spirit come down from heaven as a dove and remain on him. And I myself did not know him, but the one who sent me to baptize with water told me, 'The man on whom you see the Spirit come down and remain is the one who will baptize with the Holy Spirit.' I have seen and I testify that this is God's*

---

43 Matthew 3:13-17 NIV

Chosen One."[44]

The Word and the Spirit were beautifully involved in Jesus baptism. Their combined roles launched Jesus into His public ministry. The Word brought an affirmation to Him of His identity and the Spirit clothed him with power from on high.

Jesus' Temptation

Guided by the Spirit and Protected by the Word

The temptation of Jesus is documented in three of the four gospels; Matthew, Mark and Luke. As we read the accounts we learn that directly after His Baptism, Jesus goes into the Judean desert to fast and pray for 40 days and 40 nights. As He does so, the devil comes to tempt him.

What's interesting to me about Jesus' temptation story is that it is completely guided by the Spirit; The Spirit sends Him into a place where temptation will happen and then leads Him out of this place, fully anointed and empowered.

Into the desert:

> *At once the Spirit sent him out into the desert, and he was in the desert forty days, being tempted by Satan. He was with the wild animals, and angels attended him.*[45]

---

44 John 1:29-34 NIV
45 Mark 1:12-13 NIV

And out of the desert:

> *And Jesus returned in the power of the Spirit to Galilee, and a report about him went out through all the surrounding country. And he taught in their synagogues, being glorified by all.* [46]

This is such insight into the role of the Spirit; He drove Jesus into a difficult place, a place which tested the core of His very being.

Have you ever thought of the significance of Jesus' temptation? *Was it completely initiated by the devil, or did God allow it to happen for Jesus' sake? Would it matter if the temptation of Jesus didn't take place?*

For me, the fact that the Spirit led Jesus to this place (in some versions of scripture it says that the Holy Spirit *drove* Him there) says to me that this was a vital process for Jesus to go through. It was a preparation for Him to be able to fulfill His destiny of overcoming death, sin and the grave.

The Spirit didn't just lead him there and leave—the Spirit was guiding His complete journey. We are given this striking image of Jesus leaving with the Spirit, completely empowered and ready for ministry. They go in together and they leave together.

The Word is also a hero in this story. Jesus is guided by the

---

[46] Luke 4:14-15 NIV

Spirit, but in His weakest moments He's protected by the Word. His rebuff to all the accusations and temptations thrown His way are *"It is written..."*. His knowledge of the written Word gives Him power to overcome. This is a testament to the power of the Word. There are many things that we fight with when we're strong; our intellect, our reasoning, our emotions. But when we're stripped down, when all our strength is depleted, what's left that has power to overcome? God's Word.

Jesus' temptation in the desert is another window into how the Word and Spirit helped Him in his life.

Jesus' Ministry

He harnessed the power of the Word and the Spirit in all areas of His ministry.

Jesus is the example of how the average Christian should live. One of my heroes is Pastor Bill Johnson of Bethel Church in Redding, California. Bill's teaching has had a huge impact upon me. I remember being struck by a profound but simple message that he spoke about one time. It was a reminder that Jesus' life on Earth was there to show us what is possible; what a Christian's life can and should look like.

In that moment, Bill reminded me of how easy it is for Christians to count themselves *out* of the standard that Jesus set. People think "well Jesus was the Son of God, of course *He* could live like that!" Bill's teaching hammered home the point that Jesus – although being the Son of God – chose to come to Earth to live in a human body, limiting himself to live like a person who had full access to the Holy Spirit and the Word of the Father. In fact, Jesus lived a life with the resources that are available to every Christian today. That is a challenging truth.

It's from this place – a man with full access to God's Spirit – that He ministered. Miracles, profound teaching, healings, radical love, salvation and deliverance ensued.

His life should be a charge to us. There should be a growing appetite in us to follow His ways.

For me, the aspiration to live like Jesus has been a huge part of life. I've wrestled with what this looks like in Western culture. I've pursued healing through prayer many times. I'm drawn to and challenged by stories of people who choose to live a different way; like Shane Claiborne whose heart for community living and care for the poor oozes *Jesus*. I've read countless Christian books on faith, intimacy and love. All of these teachings and people's examples have been significant in shaping my journey.

But one thing that I've found for myself, just from reading the Bible, is how Jesus used the Word and the Spirit in all aspects of His ministry. He understood the power of the Word and Spirit and He harnessed that power and brought breakthrough.

The Spirit's Impact on Jesus' Ministry

We've already seen that Jesus was anointed by the Holy Spirit. But what did that really mean for Him? How did this anointing of the Spirit effect His ministry?

Jesus' ministry was dynamic. He healed whole towns and villages.[47] He had authority over demons and cast them out of people that been held captive for decades.[48] He raised the dead.[49] He taught with unearthly wisdom and had insight into the mysteries of the universe.

All of these things and more were a consequence of Him being anointed by and walking with the Holy Spirit in every moment of every day.

It was the Spirit that gave Him authority. It was the Spirit that gave him wisdom. It was the Spirit that gave Him knowledge. The Spirit gave Him insight and power. Why? Because these are the traits of the Holy Spirit, and the Holy Spirit abided in Him. As Jesus was filled and anointed by the Spirit, He was able to access these all these attributes as He was led from person to person and town to town.

Jesus had an understanding that a moment by moment interaction was needed with the Spirit. This anointing of the Spirit wasn't a once-off happening. The anointing of the Spirit simply meant that the Spirit was resting on Jesus. He was there with Him as a great friend, partner and helper. Interaction with the Spirit was critical as Jesus moved throughout His day. Because it was the Spirit that gave Jesus what He needed for each encounter.

This is why we see it was no one-size-fits-all approach as

---

47   Matthew 9:35
48   Mark 5:1-20
49   Luke 7:11-17, Mark 5:21-43, John 11:1-44

He ministered to people. Jesus knew that partnership was vital and following the Spirit's lead was the key to seeing the kingdom of heaven break through into the 'now'. Jesus wasn't following a manual, He was following the Spirit. He was listening to the Spirit's wisdom and direction for every single person He ministered to.

And so we see story after story of Jesus breaking through the natural realm in His ministry. Food multiplies.[50] A Woman is told the secrets of her heart.[51] An abundance of fish are caught on the other side of the boat.[52] A daughter is raised from the dead.[53] Blind men receive sight.[54] Scholars are silenced by the wisdom of His parables.[55] Storms are calmed.[56] Water is turned into wine.[57]

This was the impact that the Spirit had upon Jesus' ministry. He gave Jesus the right gift for each unique situation the Jesus faced.

The Word's Impact upon Jesus' Ministry

When it comes to Jesus' ministry, He used both the written Word and the prophetic Word to bring advancement of the Kingdom of Heaven.

---

50 Matthew 14:13-21
51 John 4:1-42
52 John 21:1-14
53 Mark 5:21-43
54 Mark 8:22-26
55 Matthew 22:34
56 Mark 4:35-41
57 John 2:1-11

His knowledge of the scriptures was outstanding. So much so that the Jewish scholars marveled at him as He taught without any formal training.[58] We see that He was dedicated to learning the Word from a young age as we have the account of him asking questions of the temple doctors as a boy.

The written Word of God becomes part of Jesus' ministry through His teaching and frequent references to scripture in all sorts of encounters.

There are those today as there were those in Jesus' day who wrongly assume that the Old Testament Scripture had no relevance when compared to the revelation of Jesus Himself. But Jesus counteracts this stance strongly with how He models scripture being integrated into His ministry and also teaching how scripture is not *separate*, but instead a *foundation* for the things to come.

> *Do not think that I have come to abolish the Law or the Prophets; I have not come to abolish them but to fulfill them.*[59]

Jesus not only models the written Word in His ministry, but He also regularly uses the prophetic Word. And as He does so we see the huge impact that follows. Perhaps the most well known story that depicts this is His encounter with the Samaritan woman he met at Jacob's well. This story is brought to us in the gospel of John and controversially shows Jesus

---

58 John 7:14
59 Matthew 5:17 NIV

to be someone who candidly steps over cultural barriers by asking this woman to draw him a drink from the well. He begins a tantalizing conversation with her about living water and never being thirsty. Then He throws her a curve ball—His prophetic word to her about her past husbands cuts through her unbelief like a hot knife through butter. Finally He reveals to her that He is the Christ, the Messiah. Her conversion is a powerful one as she not only receives the truth of who Jesus is for herself, she takes that back to her community, where many become believers.

> *Many of the Samaritans from that town believed in him because of the woman's testimony, "He told me everything I ever did." So when the Samaritans came to him, they urged him to stay with them, and he stayed two days. And because of his words many more became believers. They said to the woman, "We no longer believe just because of what you said; now we have heard for ourselves, and we know that this man really is the Savior of the world."* [60]

As we reflect and learn from Jesus' ministry and try to become like Him, it's vital we see the Word and the Spirit's role. If we're able to be a person of both the Word and the Spirit, we become tangibly close to representing Jesus' ministry to the world.

---

60   John 4: 39-42 NIV

Jesus' Death & Resurrection

He fulfilled the Word and was raised by the Spirit

The ultimate monumental happening of Jesus' life was, of course, his death and resurrection. This was the seminal event by which the entirety of human history would be changed. It was the turning point that defeated the grave and robbed death of its sting by having one who was sinless lay down His life and pay the price for many. It was His known path; the very thing He had to endure to get to the joy that was set before Him.

There was a huge prophetic lead up to these epic events of Jesus life. His death and resurrection was a prophecy that was whispered throughout the Old Testament and proclaimed by Jesus himself in the New Testament.[61]

There are over 300 prophecies in the Old Testament about the Messiah, and many of these were about His death and resurrection. Here's a small selection written hundreds of years before Jesus' death and resurrection.

> *But He was pierced through for our transgressions, He was crushed for our iniquities; The chastening for our well-being fell upon Him, And by His scourging we are healed.*[62]

> *For dogs have surrounded me; A band of evildoers has*

---

[61] Matthew 20:17-19
[62] Isaiah 53:5 ESV

encompassed me; They pierced my hands and my feet.[63]

Therefore, I will allot Him a portion with the great, And He will divide the booty with the strong; Because He poured out Himself to death, And was numbered with the transgressors; Yet He Himself bore the sin of many, And interceded for the transgressors.[64]

They divide my garments among them, And for my clothing they cast lots.[65]

For you will not leave My soul among the dead or allow your holy one to rot in the grave.[66]

These prophecies paved the way and built a spiritual momentum of truth that ultimately became a reality for humankind when He was raised from the grave.

Jesus' death and resurrection was the hour of victory for the Word. It was the point when Jesus fulfilled the Word that had been proclaimed for so many years. It was the grand occasion in which the Word had become actualized.

But the Holy Spirit was right in the middle of this history-changing event also. His role was both hugely painful and gloriously triumphant as the realization of the Father's plan unfolded.

---

63   Psalm 22:16 NASB
64   Isaiah 53:12 NASB
65   Psalm 22:18 NASB
66   Psalm 16:10 NLT

One big question I've always had is *what was the Holy Spirit's role in Jesus death?* For anyone who's had to walk a loved one through the journey of dying, they know how gut-wrenching the process is. It calls out a selflessness that longs to bring the dying person comfort and strength. But it's also marked by a feeling of powerlessness—a knowledge that you cannot stop this from happening.

At the age of 16, my grandmother – the same one that wrote those tender letters to me as an 8 year old – was told she had 6 months to live. She was 70 years old and had pancreatic cancer. My father decided it would be best if she came to live and ultimately die in our family home, and so we set up the downstairs room for her. Our main focus as her family was to make this last part of her journey comfortable and secure. It was a hard time but we walked that journey with her, giving her the strength to not fear, but to trust in Jesus.

I was actually there the moment of her departure. She'd suffered, her body was now only skin and bones, she'd been plagued by nightmares and fears but as I watched her last breath a peace came over her entire face. I honestly remember her face shining with glory, she looked straight past me with a glint of joy in her eyes and whispered *"Jesus"*. And she was gone.

I remember feeling empty, but relieved. The suffering had ended and now the joy for her had come.

The Holy Spirit had to go on a harrowing journey with Jesus as His embraced death. He had to experience the same conflict that we experience of walking His beloved through pain and suffering, knowing that it had to be done and yet longing to ease the pain. I can only imagine how much comfort and strength the Spirit brought Jesus during the Garden of Gethsemane and His walk to the cross—a hidden moment shared by only Him and Jesus.

But ultimately the Spirit's most painful moment came when the sin of the whole world that Jesus took upon Himself separated the Father and the Spirit from Jesus for the first time in history.

> *From noon until three in the afternoon darkness came over all the land. About three in the afternoon Jesus cried out in a loud voice, "Eli, Eli, lema sabachthani?" (which means "My God, my God, why have you forsaken me?").* [67]

Separation from our loved ones brings so much grief. God knows exactly what that feels like; He embraced it so that ultimately we could all have reunion with Him and each other into eternal life. Jesus, The Holy Spirit and the Father's painful separation paved the way for my grandmother's joy as she continued into eternal life. Upon the moment of her death she saw joy instead of pain, peace instead of fear. She experienced the fruit of Christ's sacrifice.

The Holy Spirit's role didn't end in grief, instead He became victorious with Jesus and the Father as He raised Jesus from the grave. We're told of the Spirit's part in Jesus resurrection by Paul in the book of Romans;

---

67 Matthew 27:45-46 NIV

> *And if the Spirit of him who raised Jesus from the dead is living in you, he who raised Christ from the dead will also give life to your mortal bodies because of his Spirit who lives in you.*[68]

How Jesus was raised from death and what exactly happened in the spiritual realms during those three days of the grave remain part mystery to us. I'm sure the detailed history will be revealed and celebrated in heaven. What we do know though is that the Father, the Spirit and Jesus Himself somehow contributed to the miracle of resurrection. They the Godhead, through love's sacrifice, defeated death and brought freedom from the fear of death.

> *Since the children have flesh and blood, he too shared in their humanity so that by his death he might break the power of him who holds the power of death—that is, the devil and free those who all their lives were held in slavery by their fear of death.*[69]

As we look to this epic part of history it's clear how the Word and the Spirit were integral to the momentum that brought salvation to all.

The life of Jesus is our standard. He's our cornerstone upon which we should build our lives from. How He lived, what

---

[68] Romans 8:11 NIV
[69] Hebrews 2: 14-15 NIV

was important to Him, and what He modeled should be important for us as we wrestle with what a Christian life should look like. I hope this chapter has given you some insight in how the Word and the Spirit worked in unison in the life of Jesus and how – if we're to be like Jesus – we need to embrace the Word and the Spirit in our lives.

5
indivisible

In this chapter I want to focus on the Word and Spirit; specifically looking at why division of these two creates a huge deficit to the Christian and to the Church. When it comes to the division of the Word and the Spirit, one of the most disheartening concerns is how much we could be missing out by keeping these apart. In this chapter I want to look at four reasons why I believe we should keep them together.

1. The Word & Spirit are in a Committed Relationship

The Word and Spirit are in a relationship—and this is essential to understand. It's a divine, committed, interactive alliance. One doesn't go to work without the other, and each one serves each other's purpose. Their overarching cause is to bring people of every tribe and tongue into a redeemed relationship with the Father, which is why the Word that is scripture is actually Spirit breathed, or the Word made flesh (Jesus) was Spirit conceived, or the Word that is now (prophecy) is Spirit gifted.

Perhaps the best Earthly analogy to describe the relationship that exists between the Word and the Spirit is a marriage.

There is a divine seal that interlocks them with the same purpose and goal. They have their unique roles and yet they are also one. And they fill the Earth with offspring that carry the DNA of both.

The whole concept of separating the two is actually nonsense—it's impossible to separate this work of God. People who think they're separating the Word and the Spirit are actually just ignoring one's existence or denying the other's presence. This doesn't change the reality though that *the Word and the Spirit are divinely connected* and constantly interweaving to glorify the Father's cause.

To deny one is an affront to God

> *Therefore what God has joined together, let no one separate.*[70]

Generally in society there is a great respect for marriage. People go to great lengths to include both partners in conversation, decision making and socializing. But let me ask a question for you married folks. *Have you ever been in a position where you're with your partner and you are being ignored by a third party? Treated as if you simply don't exist?* If you have, you'll join with me in knowing that it's one of the most dishonoring things someone can do. It's an act that overrides the couples overt desire to be seen 'together' and usually both partners find this behavior weird and insulting.

When we choose to ignore either the Word or the Spirit and

---

[70] Mark 10:9 NIV

deny their relevance, we've got to understand what an affront this is to God. It's a pious act that dismisses their love to be together and I believe this grieves the heart of God.

So the first reason why we shouldn't attempt to divide the Word and Spirit is simple but profound, they're meant to be together. Just like we wouldn't want to divide a husband and wife out of respect for their committed union, we need to pay a healthy respect to what God has joined.

2. The Word and the Spirit are Essential to Christian Growth

If you are someone who wants to grow and mature as a Christian, then it's imperative that the Word and the Spirit are part of your daily journey. It's no good having one without the other.

It's interesting what Jesus says about the Word and the Spirit. One of the most striking analogies is how He likens them to food and drink.

The Word is likened to daily bread;

> *But He answered and said, "It is written, 'Man shall not live by bread alone, but by every word that proceeds from the mouth of God.'"* [71]

---

71   Matthew 4:4 NASB

And the Spirit is likened to living water;

> *On the last day, that great day of the feast, Jesus stood and cried out, saying, "If anyone thirsts, let him come to Me and drink. He who believes in Me, as the Scripture has said, out of his heart will flow rivers of living water." But this He spoke concerning the Spirit, whom those believing in Him would receive; for the Holy Spirit was not yet given, because Jesus was not yet glorified.* [72]

Living in western society where food and drink are available in ample supply and variety, I've often taken for granted it's importance in our lives. When my son Titus was just nine months old however I had a sharp upsetting experience with him where the obvious was brought to my attention, that food and drink are vital to life, health and growth.

Titus Raphael Lorensson is my joy. He's my first-born and in those early months I was riding those stormy and spectacular waters of learning how to become a parent. Sheer joy and complete terror gripped my heart at the same time as I was overwhelmed that this gorgeous little person was in my care.

When he was around nine months old he got sick. He developed a terrible cough that wouldn't let him feed. For the first few days I wasn't that concerned, these things happen after all! But as the days went on I became increasingly concerned that he wasn't getting any food or liquid. Literally everything I gave him came back up. I phoned the doctor

---

[72] John 7: 37-39 NKJV

only to be told that it would pass. After 5 days of this, my bouncy little boy was losing weight, weak and not himself. I sat in the doctor's office in tears as I felt completely powerless. One of my main jobs as mom was to feed this little boy and I couldn't get anything in him. Finally after 9 days of barely eating anything his little limp body began accepting food and drink again.

This experience taught me a number of things. Firstly it gave me insight into my role as a mother. I cannot quite express how obsessed I became in that time about how much food and drink Titus was getting, I watched every mouthful. I knew at the end of each day how much progress he had made. I've never felt so protective over someone. I felt like a lioness pacing up and down, fiercely vigilant over this process of how much food Titus was getting. God also taught me something about growth through this incident, specifically Christian growth.

In this experience it was obvious to me that unless Titus got food and drink in his system he was not going to keep growing. In fact, not only would he stop growing, but he would waste away. I could cuddle him, I could kiss him, I could give him all the attention and affirmation I could give but none of that would actually make his body better. The only thing that would make him thrive physically was food and drink.

When it comes to discipleship, growing to be a follower of Jesus, this truth applies. Spiritual food and drink is what makes Christians grow.

Many churches have rightly accepted the importance of community, relationship and love. Sayings like 'belong before you believe' can be a frequent good message of churches today. Leaders have realized the power of family. Being loved in a church is certainly important, having deep relationships with fellow believers in community create an ideal environment for a Christian to grow. But the environment alone doesn't actually do the growing. It just creates the best possible chance for optimal growth. What actually causes growth is food and drink, or in spiritual terms, the Word and the Spirit. No matter how much we belong, no matter how much we are loved by others, no matter how great our environment is without the Word and the Spirit in our lives as Christians (daily) we will not grow.

This has huge implications for churches who out of fear of 'others' expressions barely mention the Spirit to their members and instead proudly focus on the Word. And for those who are pursuing the things of the Spirit but very rarely apply the Word, can you imagine only choosing either food or drink to live? Those who refused to drink would soon be dead and those who refused food would lose their strength and remain weak.

This is why we need to cut through the fears, misunderstandings and confusion surrounding both of these areas and make sure that they are in our daily lives so we become healthy growing Christians.

3. The Word and the Spirit are Essential to Christian Mission

> *Then Jesus came to them and said, "All authority in heaven and on earth has been given to me. Therefore go and make disciples of all nations, baptizing them in the name of the Father and of the Son and of the Holy Spirit, and teaching them to obey everything I have commanded you. And surely I am with you always, to the very end of the age."* [73]

Not only does the Word and Spirit impact Christian growth but it also has an effect on mission. Our mission is to make disciples of all nations. To do that we need to represent Jesus, which means we need to let Him be seen through our lives. Once people have seen and chosen to accept Jesus, we need to help them grow.

The famous scripture in John 13:35 emphasizes that to make Jesus visible to the World our most powerful strategy will be our love for one another and our unity together. Division and hatred between churches and Christians has the potential to blur people's understanding and vision of who Jesus is. If we harbor division among ourselves between the Word and the Spirit we potentially dilute the effectiveness of the mission of the church.

We also know that in order to grow spiritually and to grow others we need the Word and the Spirit present daily, just like food and drink. The Word and the Spirit are vital for

---

[73] Matthew 28: 16-20 NIV

discipleship. If there's weak discipleship, ultimately there will be weak mission because discipleship is God's plan for the mission movement of the church.

I believe that the more we see the Word & Spirit held together in a Christian or a church or a movement, the more we will see the mission of Christ's Church impact the world. Christians will be stronger in their own faith and the Jesus that the church represents to the world will become crystal clear.

One of the most inspiring pieces of literature that I've read on why we should strive to bring the Word and the Spirit together is a prophetic piece attributed to Smith Wigglesworth in 1947—just a few years before his death. This is part of the extract:

> *During the next few decades there will be two distinct moves of the Holy Spirit across the church in Great Britain. The first move will affect every church that is open to receive it and will be characterized by a restoration of the baptism and gifts of the Holy Spirit. The second move of the Holy Spirit will result in people leaving historic churches and planting new churches. In the duration of each of these moves, the people who are involved will say 'This is the great revival'. But the Lord says 'No, neither is this the great revival but both are steps towards it.*
>
> *When the new church phase is on the wane, there will be evidenced in the churches something that has not been seen before: a coming together of those with an emphasis on the Word and those with an emphasis on the Spirit.*

When the Word and the Spirit come together, there will be the biggest movement of the Holy Spirit that the nation, and indeed the world, has ever seen. It will mark the beginning of a revival that will eclipse anything that has been witnessed within these shores, even the Wesleyan and the Welsh revivals of former years. The outpouring of God's Spirit will flow over from the UK to the mainland of Europe, and from there will begin a missionary move to the ends of the earth.[74]

If you're a big picture type of person this could get you inspired. If you dream of worldwide mission, then this could make you stop and think. For me, when I happened upon this prophecy many years ago, it struck a chord in my heart. *Could it be that the coming together of the Word and the Spirit would have such an impact on mission?*

For some this could easily be written off as sensationalism. A big dramatic consequence that happens when these churches come together could seem to some as mystical nonsense. But let's just stop and unpack this.

We're talking about mission and revival—millions of people worldwide becoming Christians. We've already seen that there's a unique revelation that comes to people who don't know Christ when they see Christians come together in love. Should it surprise us that if there was a move into unity on the Word & the Spirit that many more people would see Jesus?

74   byfaith.co.uk

Also, we've looked at how vital the Word and the Spirit is in the growth of the Christian. As Christians grow, they're more able to help others grow. Should it surprise us that when the Word and the Spirit are in place and at work in the average Christian and in the average church that we should see many more come into the kingdom?

Lastly, if there's ever an experience where the Word and the Spirit are inseparable, it's when a person becomes a Christian—the experience of being born again. Every Christian – whether they like to admit it or not – started out with the Word and the Spirit birthing their eternal life. Jesus talked about this great mystery when He spoke to Nicodemus:

> *Now there was a Pharisee, a man named Nicodemus who was a member of the Jewish ruling council. He came to Jesus at night and said, "Rabbi, we know that you are a teacher who has come from God. For no one could perform the signs you are doing if God were not with him." Jesus replied, "Very truly I tell you, no one can see the kingdom of God unless they are born again." "How can someone be born when they are old?" Nicodemus asked. "Surely they cannot enter a second time into their mother's womb to be born!" Jesus answered, "Very truly I tell you, no one can enter the kingdom of God unless they are born of water and the Spirit. Flesh gives birth to flesh, but the Spirit gives birth to spirit. You should not be surprised at my saying, 'You must be born again.*[75]

---

[75] John 3:1-7 NIV

The Word is our foundation, it's the gospel, Jesus made flesh, God's offer of love to humanity. When a person accepts this offer, the Holy Spirit comes and gives new life to them, re-birthing them into the family of God. Even though it could take an eternity for us to get our heads around this dynamic, would it surprise us that when these two vital parts of our faith are joined in His church, we would see a multitude of people becoming Christians?

Maybe what Smith Wigglesworth prophesied just makes sense in the fact that this could be the fruit of spiritual synergy. Like all prophecy, this word has to be weighed and wrestled with. The question I ask myself with a prophetic word like this is *"Is this a prediction or is this an offer?"* If it's a prediction, great! But if it's an offer then we need to get behind the vision and take God up on it.

4. The Word and the Spirit Bring Life to the Full

As a young adult I had a season of my life where I rejected God, His Church and my whole Christian background. I think many young people go through this, especially when they've been brought up in a strictly religious setting. There were a few different triggers for me, but the main one was my parents' divorce.

At the age of 17 my parents marriage started crumbling before my eyes. This led me to question everything. As a young idealist I couldn't reconcile how a professed Christian couple could let their marriage go. I was harboring a religious spirit.

As time went on I learned about life, grace and human nature, and as a result I gained more compassion and understanding for when things go wrong.

There was very little in that time that could have penetrated the walls I'd put up around my heart, but I remember one verse that seemed to stick out. It was a verse in the gospel of John—something that Jesus himself declared:

> *The thief comes only to steal and kill and destroy; I have come that they may have life, and have it to the full.* [76]

This idea that Jesus came to bring life in all its fullness was a refreshing concept to me which seemed to go against the boring grind of religion that I'd been used to.

This verse was compelling to me... *life to the full.* Really?

So much of what I'd been brought up with was well-meaning religion. As a twenty-year-old I was up for 'life to the full', but my approach in finding by flirting with the party scene in my hometown of Cardiff didn't seem to be working.

Now, in looking back over the years of pursuing faith in Jesus, I've come to know how fundamentally important this verse is to the Christian life. I've met so many people who assume that the offer of Christianity is all about *escape of hell and access to heaven* in some far and distant future. But my own understanding of what Christ offered was a *redemption* of life

[76] John 10:10 NIV

that starts the moment you give your life to Jesus. He came to bring fullness of life today, tomorrow, through death and into eternity.

I've also come to know how instrumental the Word and the Spirit are in fulfilling Jesus' promise of life to the full. This is my final reason why I believe we need to hold the Word and the Spirit together. If you've accepted Jesus as your Lord and Savior then you need to embrace the Word and the Spirit to have life to the full.

What does Life to the Full Look Like?

If you asked the average person what life to the full looks like, I wonder what responses you'd get. I imagine people would say things like; good family life or relationships, financial security, wealth, fulfillment of dreams, freedom, security or peace. The list could go on and on.

It's quite a good idea to think about what Jesus meant by 'life to the full'. When I think about it, I believe there can be many aspects of life to the full which depend on personal preferences. But when I think of *what it means to be human and what really matters*, I've whittled it down to six important things: love, security, freedom, joy, purpose and power.

I want to explore with you how the Word and the Spirit work together to bring these areas into fruition within the life of a Christian.

Life to the Full: *Love*

> *The greatest thing you'll ever learn is just to love and be loved in return.*[77]

Love is a fundamental part of being human. We have a built-in drive to love and be loved—whether we like it or not. Love is expressed and needed through many relationships; parents, grandparents, siblings, wider family, friends and ultimately with a life partner.

We have an inherent need for love which causes us to do some of our best and worst things. When we have it in it's pure form, it makes us overcomers and it's books are the hero stories of our history. It trumps selfishness, shapes our character and chooses to serve others.

But even with our best intentions, love in the human heart can be tainted. In our world there's a constant war on love. It's purity is persistently challenged by other fleshly desires, and it slips too easily from our grasp.

Even after all of that, it still amazes me that love is what most people believe in—regardless of their faith. A huge amount of people around the world believe love is the answer to a whole host of problems. The movement of love is strong and alive today. This is excellent news because the God of the Christian faith is Love Himself, and the key to seeing love explode across the world is to know Him.

---

77 'Nature Boy' Eden Ahbez

The Bible sheds it's own wisdom on love. It fully backs the belief that love should be the most prominent force. For Christians, the central command from Jesus is to *love God with everything and to love our neighbor as ourself.*

> *And you shall love the Lord your God with all your heart, with all your soul, with all your mind, and with all your strength.'This is the first commandment. And the second, like it, is this: 'You shall love your neighbor as yourself.' There is no other commandment greater than these.*[78]

It's a potent command that aims at transforming life on earth by mirroring heaven's value system. The Word and the Spirit are indispensable helpers in our pursuit of this command, and in our reach for God's standard of love.

Love from God

Loving God with all your heart, soul, mind and strength can seem a little overwhelming. Especially as we can so easily fail to love the people around us on a daily basis. Human wisdom on the topic of love rests on the ability to choose love over other things. It's a self-discipline that is certainly good and true to some level. It's choosing to believe in love even when we don't feel it or choosing the way of love over other attractive options. People practice this discipline everyday. Sometimes they win and sometimes they fail. While this human pursuit of love amidst so much adversity is admirable, it can lead to feelings of striving.

---

78   Mark 12:30-31 ESV

The Bible discloses a truth about love that undercuts the notion that *we just need to try harder.* Instead, it talks of love as a wellspring of life.

The wellspring of love is God Himself. Without first receiving His love, it's impossible to truly give it. So the whole beginning of love's heroic crusade comes from our ability to receive the love of God.

We love Him because He first loved us. [79]

This is where we begin see the amazing work of the Word and the Spirit taking action. They are both instrumental in allowing us to know and experience the love of God.

The Word Reveals the Father's love

The major purpose of the Word is to reveal God's love to us. It's not just that God *is* love, but that also *He passionately loves us.* Whether it's scripture, the life of Jesus or the prophetic word, the theme is as strong as ever—a huge announcement to the Earth and all it's inhabitants that *God is love,* and His love for us is beyond our comprehension.

The Word that is scripture paints a grand masterpiece of the big story of God and humanity. The problems are raised of sin and corruption through broad strokes, and God's answers are given through sacrifice and atonement obtained by Jesus' life, death and resurrection.

---

79   1 John 4:19 NKJV

The details in scripture, the language used, parables told and knowledge given all constantly reaffirm God's story of love.

Jesus' life reveals glimpses of how the Trinity interact in love. Each one honors the other—a perfect union is between them. The founding fathers of the Christian faith described this relationship of the trinity as *perichoresis*. This is a Greek word that alludes to *an eternal dance of love between the Father, Son and Holy Spirit.*

Scripture also places God's desires firmly within family. He is depicted as a Father. Not just any Father, but the best one we could possibly imagine; one that is always looking for His kids wherever they are in life. Kids that are lost. Kids that have rebelled. Kids that are by His side. And we are known as His children.

The Word made flesh—Jesus, is the biggest revelation of the love of God to humanity. The infamous verse that's captured so many hearts says it like this:

> *For God so loved the world that He gave His only begotten Son, that whoever believes in Him should not perish but have everlasting life.* [80]

Here we see a God who doesn't just talk the talk but walks the walk. His passion for us to be in loving relationship with Him becomes the joy that helps Him endure the cross. He's willing to do whatever it takes to get His kids back.

---

80 John 3:16 NKJV

Jesus talks to His disciples about this extraordinary type of love:

> *Greater love has no one than this, than to lay down one's life for his friends.* [81]

Here the Word made flesh becomes the greatest display of God's love for mankind.

We continue to see today how God's prophetic Word fulfills this very purpose of revealing the love of God. The prophetic Word brings this revelation to our front door. Just in case we cannot comprehend how the love of God is for us *individually,* the prophetic knocks down the door and presents us with our own personalized invitation.

The Spirit allows us to Experience the Father's Love

It's quite amazing that the Father's love has been revealed to us. Knowing about the Father's love is one thing, but experiencing it is quite another.

In a relationship it's important that we know and experience love. With my daughter Penny, I tell her I love her everyday, especially each night as she goes to sleep. She will grow up knowing that her mom loves her. But I also very naturally spend copious amounts of time holding her, kissing her, laughing with her, buying her cute outfits and expressing my love to her. She's not only *told* of my love, she *experiences* it.

---

[81] John 15: 13 NKJV

The same is true about the love of God. The astounding truth is that God wants us to know and experience His love. He has gone to great lengths to *communicate* on many levels that He loves us, but He also expresses His love to us through the Holy Spirit so we can experience that love.

> *And hope does not put us to shame, because God's love has been poured out into our hearts through the Holy Spirit, who has been given to us.* [82]

The way we experience God's love through the Holy Spirit is certainly not one-size-fits-all. We each have 'love languages' and God – who is more in tune with our character than anyone else we could ever know – will love us individually in our own language.

Some of us we will feel His presence, others will know His provision. To some His humor will be instrumental and yet others will need to experience His hold. His words of affirmation are so important to some people, while others will feel His love by receiving His gifts. These are just some of the ways the Holy Spirit works to express the love of God. No one person will have the same relationship with Him as the other. God, who encompasses perfect love, will interweave throughout the seasons of our life and express His perfect love to us through the Spirit.

It's important to know the nature of these experiences of love. Some experiences can be monumental, and others will be the

[82] Romans 5:5 NIV

everyday kisses from God—just as in our human relationships we have a few big moments of love and many little ones along the way.

When my son was born I was overwhelmed by the experience of love I felt for Him. Nothing can ever quite prepare you for your first born. In his first week I was almost scared at the amount of love that had consumed my heart for this little fella. I remember saying to his godmother and my best friend Netty *"Oh no, what have I done! I now have this love in me and I will never be the same!"*

That was a monumental moment for Titus and I. When I look to the future I'm sure there will be many more big experiences of love that we'll share along the way; graduation, marriage, his own children. But if I experienced that level of intensity every day I'd simply be exhausted and get nothing done. If I looked to that first week of getting to know my son as the standard, I could easily fall into disillusionment and, more seriously, miss out on the sweet everyday encounters of love happening between us.

These small touches of love are equally important to me as a mother. Like the other day when he came to me with his 5 year old thoughts and said "I'm so proud of you mommy." Was it as dramatic as that first week? No, but it stole my heart, and my heart gets warmed everyday by his sweet presence.

We need to know that the Holy Spirit expresses the love of God to us in similar rhythms of life. There will be big monumental times sprinkled between many more everyday moments of love. To fully embrace God's love we need to accept and appreciate all encounters, both big and small.

As we gain an understanding of the Father's love and daily experience it our capacity to love others increases. We begin the adventure of what it means to love God with all our lives and have the privilege of turning the world upside down by being able to love others like we love ourselves.

Our Love for One Another

Life to the full really kicks into gear when we start loving one another. Loving each other from the eternal source of love Himself is a game changer. It messes with the momentum of a self-centered society and from it, all the systems of this world can be redeemed.

The Word and Spirit are continually encouraging us to take full advantage of the fact that we have the eternal life-giving source of love in us. This love from God that we daily receive has a forceful destiny to flow out from our lives to others around us. We have a never ending supply of love to give—we need never run dry because of the love of God.

Unfortunately, even after we receive God's love we can still carry the habits of someone who has lived in deficit. After all, habits are hard to break. Before knowing the wealth of God's love, most of us relate to others with a limited resource. During that time, habits are formed to self protect and guard love. It takes the revelation and reinforced encouragement of the Word and Spirit to break these habits that come from poverty.

It's a process for us to live out the full weight of this truth—that the love of God has made us rich people with no limits and no boundaries.

As we study scripture we are strongly encouraged to love one another:

> *Dear friends, let us love one another, for love comes from God. Everyone who loves has been born of God and knows God. Whoever does not love does not know God, because God is love. This is how God showed his love among us: He sent his one and only Son into the world that we might live through him. This is love: not that we loved God, but that he loved us and sent his Son as an atoning sacrifice for our sins. Dear friends, since God so loved us, we also ought to love one another. No one has ever seen God; but if we love one another, God lives in us and his love is made complete in us.* [83]

Perhaps this is because *to love others with full abandonment* can be one of the most satisfying things to do with one's life. Maybe it's because our love leaves an eternal legacy while other efforts whither away. *Loving God with all our hearts and others like ourselves* is one of the wisest things we can do with our lives. The Word and the Spirit are integral to this process bringing revelation, experience and a capacity within us to give our love away.

---

83   1 John 4: 7-12 NIV

Life to the Full: *Security*

In the first few years of becoming a Christian it was as if God's whole purpose for me was to re-establish my security. I remember those times fondly. There was no big rush for ministry or for me to do anything. It was more about learning how to be me. He was working with me at a pace that was right for me. I remember envisioning my life as a building made of bricks, as if God was gently taking me apart brick by brick and then putting me back together in the most masterful way. All of this could appear like a painful process, but it was actually very gentle. I was aware that this was a process; God was re-establishing me, my core identity, my true personality and ultimately my purpose. I'd been spiritually re-born into a new family, and my identity was slowly being established as a child of God.

Security is such an integral part of 'life to the full'. Insecure people tend to spend so much energy on their insecurities that can become very difficult to feel free and experience the joy of life. This was me for many years. I had many reasons to be insecure coming from a broken family. The security that came with accepting Jesus was an amazing gift to me.

But even those whose lives have been relatively easy and safe, the human version of security can only go so deep. Most people carry deep questions of *Who am I? Where do I fit in? Am I safe?* at various times of their lives.

So what part do the Word and Spirit play in establishing this security?

The Word - A Solid Foundation

Some of you might remember an old Sunday school song about the wise and foolish man:

> *The wise man built his house upon the rock*
> *The wise man built his house upon the rock*
> *The wise man built his house upon the rock*
> *And the rain came tumbling down*
>
> *Oh, the rain came down*
> *And the floods came up*
> *The rain came down*
> *And the floods came up*
> *The rain came down*
> *And the floods came up*
> *And the wise man's house stood firm.*

Later on in the song we see the foolish man's house that was built on the sand fall flat in the midst of the storm. It's a simple song stating the importance of a firm foundation. Jesus is the rock. But how do you build your house upon the rock? Well, for the answer you need to return to the original parable from which the song was written. Here's one account from the gospel of Matthew:

> *Jesus said "Therefore everyone who hears these words of mine and puts them into practice is like a wise man who built his house on the rock. The rain came down, the streams rose, and the winds blew and beat against that house; yet it did not fall, because it had its foundation on the rock. But everyone who hears these words of mine and does not put*

them into practice is like a foolish man who built his house on sand. The rain came down, the streams rose, and the winds blew and beat against that house, and it fell with a great crash." [84]

Hearing God's Word and putting it into practice is how we build our house on this sure foundation. This parable is giving us a bold insight into the power of the Word—how *listening to it* and *putting it into practice* allows us to become truly secure.

This is why scripture is so important for us—it contains the teachings of Jesus, His revelation and His wisdom. As we read it and allow it to change our lives, the promise is that our security is established.

A big part of my early Christian journey was allowing myself to be challenged enough by Jesus' teachings to actually become changed by them.

I think new Christians are a blessing to any group of believers. They carry a freshness with them and a zest for truth and revelation that so often can be watered down as the years go on. I remember being so childlike in my faith as a new Christian, in the best possible way. My faith wasn't complicated at all, and this had it's merits.

In the first year after I gave my life to Jesus, I lived in a small intentional community of six. The house on Burghley road has since hosted other expressions of community life. At the time,

---

84   Matthew 7:24-27 NIV

my house-mates and I would eat together every evening and get up to pray together every morning. The house itself was a lovely Victorian semi-detached in a great part of Bristol, UK. But the house was sparsely furnished and most of us living there had little to no income. I had just started university at the time as a full-time student.

In one of the prayer meetings I remember the group talking about how much we needed furniture, so I piped in with my freshly zealous enthusiasm stating that *we should simply pray in faith for exactly what we needed because that's what the bible said we should do.* It was early in the morning and I got a few raised eyebrows, but everyone agreed to pray for the furniture. One item that was mentioned was a study desk. We prayed. Later that day my shocked house-mate came home saying that there was a free desk out on the street opposite our house. We collected it together and enjoyed the provision that faith brings.

As we study the Word and put it into practice what we're essentially doing is *building our lives on an unshakable rock.* In my early days of faith I experienced a level of excitement in simply doing what the Word said to do. As my journey has gone on, however, I've known the storms that have really tested my firm foundation; times where I'm glad of my unshakable ground. The Word of God brings this security— the rock that we build upon, and which storms can't touch.

The Word Brings The Father's Affirmation

In those early days another extremely important part of establishing my security was the revelation that God was indeed our Father. He was *my* Father—a Father whose love for His children far exceeded our limited grasp.

> *See what great love the Father has lavished on us, that we should be called children of God!* [85]

As a new Christian, I couldn't fully grasp my desperate need of His affirmation. The more I experienced of the Father's love, the more I craved His Words—as if my spirit was dry, broken ground and His Words were rain nourishing and mending my core being.

One place I found His words of affirmation were the scriptures. As I read and re-read the Bible I was nourished with the truth of His words. These words were the foundational truths that spoke of the Father God and his love, purposes and passion. As I internalized these scriptures I began to feel safe and rooted into an unshakable family.

I also started to experience the Father speak to me through the gift of prophecy. Once again during this time, these words were mainly words of affirmation; who I was and how important I was to Him. God was using His words to re-establish my true identity.

I love the way the Father affirmed Jesus at His baptism. Jesus had the foundational words of scripture, but the Father bursts in dramatically with a 'now' word of affirmation for Jesus. Here's the account in the gospel of Matthew:

---

[85] 1 John 3:1 NIV

> *As soon as Jesus was baptized, he went up out of the water. At that moment heaven was opened, and he saw the Spirit of God descending like a dove and alighting on him. And a voice from heaven said, "This is my Son, whom I love; with him I am well pleased."* [86]

It's interesting how much this continues to happen today at the beginnings of people's journeys with Jesus. The Father cannot resist speaking prophetically to His newborn kids. He showers them with His words of love and this establishes in them a sure footing, a security and a solid ground.

The Spirits Gives us a Deposit

The Spirit is always involved in establishing our security. His Spirit empowers the Word to re-establish us. Again we see that the two are inseparable in their actions.

But in this great aspect of life—our security, I love how God uses the Spirit to once again bring us complete security. The Spirit in the Bible is likened to many things, but one of my favorites is how the Bible describes the Spirit as a deposit which guarantees the promise of what's to come.

> *Now it is God who makes both us and you stand firm in Christ. He anointed us, set his seal of ownership on us, and put his Spirit in our hearts as a deposit, guaranteeing what is to come.* [87]

---

86 Matthew 3:16-17 NIV
87 2 Corinthians 1: 21-22 NIV

We recently bought our home in Fort Collins, Colorado. But here in The States, the way you buy a property means that sometimes, until the day you complete, there are no real assurances that the property is yours. Something could easily go wrong at the last minute. I remember feeling slightly anxious while waiting for confirmation of the sale of what is now our current home. The boxes were packed and we were ready to move. There was no plan B. Fortunately for us everything went smoothly.

Before that, the only time I had ever witnessed the security that a deposit brings is when I bought my first house in Bristol, UK. In England it's quite different. There's two stages of property purchase, known as exchange and completion. The exchange happens first, this is where contracts are signed between the buyer and the seller and a deposit is put down. This part is a legally binding agreement between both parties that the house will be sold/bought. During the exchange a date is assigned for completion. The completion is when all funds are transferred, the property is vacant and keys are handed over to the buyer. The completion is usually at least two weeks after the exchange. Once you exchange on a house you pretty much know it's yours even though you haven't paid in full or moved it yet.

As we accept Christ we enter into an exchange where we're now legally part of His family. The Holy Spirit is our deposit guaranteeing our future inheritance as sons and daughters of God. This deposit of the Spirit allows us to rest easy in the knowledge that it is finished. There are no last minute surprises and no uncertainties. Our future home is secure in Him.

> *Do not let your hearts be troubled. You believe in God; believe also in me. My Father's house has many rooms; if that were not so, would I have told you that I am going there to prepare a place for you? And if I go and prepare a place for you, I will come back and take you to be with me that you also may be where I am.*[88]

God wants us to be secure. It's impossible to have life in all it's fullness without some sense of security; without knowing who you are and where you fit and where your home is. It's remarkable how deeply involved the Word and the Spirit are in ensuring we get this aspect of our lives into place. They are busy at work to make sure Christians know and receive their security as children of God.

Life to the Full: *Freedom*

When we gain our spiritual security, it usually leads us to a place where we aspire to be free on the inside and out. Freedom is another pillar in the house called 'life to the full'. Security brings us to a place of clarity about who we are and what we are meant to have in our lives.

For example, before I became a Christian at the age of 21 I was completely unaware of my brokenness, my weakness and my need for healing. My insecurity was so dominant that it blinded me from these things. In fact, my insecurity fueled an outwardly confident girl that most people thought was self-assured. It was only when I gave my life to Jesus and got

---

[88] John 14: 1-3 NIV

re-built with the Word and the Spirit's help that I became sharply aware that these things in my life were actually things that should go. They weren't normal. They were things that had held me captive. The projected confidence was seen in my eyes for what it was; a false cover-up of the confused mess that was inside. As a child of God with the Father's affirmation, I now had an appetite for freedom.

The Word and the Spirit play a progressive role in the bringing about of freedom to the average believer.

The Spirit Brings Freedom

> *And because you belong to him, the power of the life-giving Spirit has freed you from the power of sin that leads to death.*[89]

The Spirit of God is integral to freedom. Paul describes this in his letter to the Corinthians:

> *Now the Lord is the Spirit, and where the Spirit of the Lord is, there is freedom.*[90]

Simply put, wherever the Spirit goes, freedom tags along. This is probably why we see a lot of inner-freedom happen in the early days of people becoming Christians. As they give their lives to Jesus they also receive the Spirit that the Bible tells us indwells in believers. A fight then ensues for freedom to

---

[89] Romans 8:2 NLT
[90] 2 Corinthians 3:17 NIV

become actualized for the person. Just *being a Christian* puts you on freedom's side.

This is also why we see healing and deliverance happen when Christians gather in worship. The Spirit of God is in us, but also can come upon us as we gather together to worship Him. Where the Spirit of the Lord is there is freedom.

The Spirit Anoints People to Minister Freedom

The Spirit first anointed Jesus. We see this unfold through his baptism, his temptation in the desert and his walk out of the desert. Luke describes this moment:

> *Jesus returned to Galilee in the power of the Spirit*[91]

Directly after this we see Jesus in the synagogue reading from the book of Isaiah:

> *The Spirit of the Lord is on me, because he has anointed me to proclaim good news to the poor. He has sent me to proclaim freedom for the prisoners and recovery of sight for the blind, to set the oppressed free.*[92]

He stuns the crowd with His declaration of who He is:

> *Then he rolled up the scroll, gave it back to the attendant and sat down. The eyes of everyone in the synagogue were*

---

91 Luke 4:14 NIV
92 Luke 4:18 NIV

fastened on him. He began by saying to them, "Today this scripture is fulfilled in your hearing." [93]

Immediately afterwards, Jesus fulfills what he's declared as He delivers a man of evil spirits in the town of Capernaum.

The most wonderful truth is that the Spirit is here to anoint people to be ministers of freedom today. Jesus modeled what it looked like. Not only does the freedom accompany the Spirit's presence, but His anointing allows people to bring breakthrough of freedom for others.

The Word Finds the Hidden Places

The Word is an active participant in bringing God's desire for freedom to each individual. One of the great privileges as a pastor is seeing breakthrough in wholeness for people. We live in a complicated, broken, sinful world. It's no surprise that the average person can carry all sorts of scars from broken families, eating disorders, promiscuous behavior, divorce, bereavement, critical words or abuse to name a few.

As Christians we can learn to handle some of the hardest experiences in life with the Holy Spirit and end up free and clear of baggage. I've been amazed as I've witnessed this first-hand with some of my closest friends and family. However, for many people who don't know how to walk through these times with God they end up surviving these hardships with a number of wounds which ultimately haunt

---

93 Luke 4:20-21 NIV

them and rob them of freedom and joy.

Some new Christians experience a sharp realization of these injuries of war, and subsequently an all out effort by the Word and the Spirit to get them cared for, cleaned up and healed.

Sometimes these wounds are hidden under the layers of life's experience. The roots of unhealthy behavior can be buried deep within a person's soul. They hide and often the person involved doesn't even know where to look. If getting someone spiritually and emotionally whole was likened to surgery, you'd need a precise diagnostic tool in the hand of a master surgeon to operate.

Amazingly, the Bible shows us that Jesus is our 'great physician' and that the Word of God is a precise and powerful tool. In Hebrews the Word is likened to a double edged sword that's famous for being able to penetrate even the hardest of places:

> *For the word of God is living and active. Sharper than any double-edged sword, it penetrates even to dividing soul and spirit, joints and marrow; it judges the thoughts and attitudes of the heart.*[94]

God continually uses His Word as an instrument to bring freedom. Sometimes scripture, sometimes the life of Jesus and sometimes a prophetic word will pinpoint a specific area that needs healing. It's laser focus gets right to the issue and is fully

---

94 Hebrews 4:12 NIV

backed with power to not just identify a wound, but also to heal it.

The Word is as Strong as Iron

> *"Is not my word like fire," declares the LORD, "and like a hammer that breaks a rock in pieces?"* [95]

Sometimes we can experience a lack of freedom in the circumstances we face. There are seasons in life that can feel like prison walls have been built up around us; we get trapped by a run of job losses, broken relationships, injustices and grief. Have you had any times like these? Where freedom seems far off? Where the odds seem stacked against you?

Well, the Word is powerfully active even in these times to break down negative mindsets and hopelessness. It's strength is legendary like a hammer that can break rock into pieces. I've seen how a Word from God can turn around even the most dire circumstances.

One of my most memorable examples was how God's Word affected my friend Simon.

Simon and his wife were going through a seriously trying time. They were surrounded by unknowns and weren't sure about their future. They weren't sure whether they would have to leave their home and their city that they'd invested in for decades.

---

95   Jeremiah 23:29 NIV

I knew that these guys were going through something but I didn't know the ins and outs. One morning God impressed upon my heart to pray for them. As I did, I immediately got a prophetic Word for them. *Iron.* I saw this word in my mind's eye—iron. *"Tell them that My will for their life is like iron"* I sensed the Father say. I spent a bit of time searching for verses in the Bible about iron and quickly crafted this email for them:

3 January 2012 11.54

Hi Guys

Happy new year!

The father prompted me today to pray for you guys and I felt Him say a few things so I thought I'd better email you both. When I was praying for you I had a word come to me straight away - that word was iron. I prayed about it and felt a number of things:

1. Firstly that God is your deliverer and anything that is imprisoning you He can break - even iron! Nothing is too strong for Him to break.
Psalm 107:16 NIV

for he breaks down gates of bronze and cuts through bars of iron.
Isaiah 45:2 NIV

I will go before you and will level the mountains; I will break down gates of bronze and cut through bars of iron.

2. Secondly, His will for your life is like iron. No man can break it. Even if it is put in the fire - it will be the father who is in control and He might reshape you but it will be for His divine purpose over your life.
Jeremiah 15:12 NIV

"Can a man break iron-- iron from the north--or bronze?"
Deuteronomy 33:24-25

About Asher he said: "Most blessed of sons is Asher; let him be favored by his brothers, and let him bathe his feet in oil. The bolts of your gates will be iron and bronze, and your strength will equal your days.

3. Thirdly, there is the odd story in the OT about the iron axe head floating - a miracle. I felt God say specifically that you were going to see a miracle this year. Also I felt Him say that where something was destined to sink (by the world's standards) you would actually see it float - which might be the miracle?
2 Kings 6:6 NIV

The man of God asked, "Where did it fall?" When he showed him the place, Elisha cut a stick and threw it there, and made the iron float.

Anyway loads of love to you. I pray all blessing and favor on your year

Ruth

A few days later I heard from Simon's wife Liz thanking me

for the encouragement. I thought that was it until two weeks later Simon came up to me almost bursting with excitement. He told me the back story:

> *Liz printed out your email and put it on the fridge because it really impacted her. I didn't even read it because I was in such a despondent mood. In the meantime we decided to listen for a word from God, so we went out to Severn beach where it's open, you know a wide space to think and pray about leaving Bristol and what to do, selling up that kind of thing. While we were there God spoke to me really specifically. He told me to get in the car and drive to a reclamation center in Bristol. He said I would find an Anvil there which would cost 60 pounds and that I was to buy it and it place it in my garden. So we get in the car drive back to bristol and go to this reclamation yard. Sure enough there is an Anvil on sale. Eventually after much procrastinating I went up to one of the guys there and asked him how much something like the Anvil would cost. Immediately he said 60 pounds. We bought it there and then. As we were driving home we looked at each other and said to one another 'ok this is a bit weird'. Then Liz asks me "what exactly is an Anvil anyhow?" I said "well it's essentially a big lump of iron", at that she looked at me and said you need to read said Ruth's prophecy.*
>
> *Simon.*

This word from God and its bizarre confirmation gave Simon and Liz the endurance they needed in a time of hopelessness. They've since told me how this word seemed to anchor them and give them strength. It smashed through the walls that surrounded them at the time and created a doorway into the future.

The Word and the Spirit long to bring us freedom. They get behind Jesus' cause of liberty and make it a reality for each believer.

Life to the Full: *Joy*

Joy is the serious business of Heaven.[96]

I believe that one of the major pieces to the *life to the full* puzzle is the ability to live in joy. Sometimes we can take everything so seriously – our thoughts, debates and missions – that we forget that God wants us to have joy. Happy, free, rejoicing Christians will speak loudly to the world. It's a testimony to the transforming power of God in our lives.

Joy is the infallible sign of the presence of God.[97]

The definition of joy has been difficult to pin down. People will say that *joy is not happiness alone, but more than happiness.* I'm inclined to agree with them, but joyful people also seem happy.

Joy, it seems, is the ultimate freedom. It's a positioning of our lives which gives us the ability to appreciate life itself. It allows us to feel alive, to breath in air, to be wowed by beauty and to

---

96 C. S Lewis, Letters to Malcolm: Chiefly on Prayer (San Diego: Harvest, 1964), 92-93.
97 Pierre Teilhard de Chardin

enjoy the blessings that God has given us.

My husband Chris and I – who are both visionary types – have commented on how challenged we feel to grasp joy at various seasons of our life. Driven people can easily fall into the trap of living in the future, and inadvertently bypass the offer to live life in joy today. Whenever we get to a point where we are grumbling, worrying or complaining we realize that we've let joy slip through our fingers and need God to reposition us.

Joy is an Outcome of the Word and Spirit

We humans aren't capable of creating joy out of thin air—joy is God given. But we can choose to follow the wisdom that God gives us regarding *where it comes from.*

Joy is a spiritual outcome of having God in our lives and allowing the Word and the Spirit to do their work in us. When we look at what the Bible says of the Word and Spirit, we can clearly see that joy is a byproduct of having embraced the Word and Spirit.

In the book of Galatians we see that joy is a fruit of the Spirit:

> *But the fruit of the Spirit is love, joy, peace, patience, kindness, goodness, faithfulness, gentleness, and self-control. Against such things there is no law.*[98]

---

98 Galatians 5:22 ESV

And in Jeremiah we see how the Word becomes the prophets joy as he eats the scroll:

> *When your words came, I ate them; they were my joy and my heart's delight, for I bear your name, LORD God Almighty.*[99]

> *I have told you this so that my joy may be in you and that your joy may be complete.*[100]

As we choose to embrace the Word and the Spirit in our daily lives, a foundation of joy is established. The security and freedom previously mentioned is a huge part of this. The more we accept God's Word and the more we walk with the Spirit, the deeper the foundation of joy becomes.

Doses of Joy

Not only does the Word and Spirit pave a foundation of joy in our lives, but they both give measures of joy at various times throughout life. God uses the Word and the Spirit to refresh and reignite our joy.

Refreshment from Scripture

In Deuteronomy there's a beautiful verse about how God's Word refreshes us like a dew, showers and abundant rain:

---

99 Jeremiah 15:16 NIV
100 John 15:11 NIV

> *Let my teaching fall like rain and my words descend like dew, like showers on new grass, like abundant rain on tender plants.*[101]

Have you ever experienced scripture doing this? A passage of God's teaching lightly resting on you with a freshness like the dew on the grass? Have you felt scripture rain upon you like a shower out of nowhere? Or just drench you with revelation like that of abundant rain? God's Word to us brings these doses of joy that reignite our spirit. His Word that is scripture can water us, invigorating our inner being.

This is one of the reasons why it's so important for us to read scripture daily. When we do, we position ourselves to receive refreshment.

The Wine of the Holy Spirit

The Holy Spirit is also likened to wine in the Bible. In the gospels, Jesus describes the new work of the Spirit to be like wine filling old vessels. This likening the Spirit to wine points to celebration and blessing, and as much as we witness the Spirit's indwelling in our daily walk with Him, there are seasons where the Spirit is poured out upon us—moments of euphoria, wonder and bliss.

> *Wise leaders should have known that the human heart cannot exist in a vacuum. If Christians are forbidden to enjoy the wine of the Spirit they will turn to the wine of the*

---

[101] Deuteronomy 32:2 NIV

flesh....Christ died for our hearts and the Holy Spirit wants to come and satisfy them.[102]

One of the most memorable times where the Spirit did this for me was when I was in a conference in Harrogate, UK. I was with the staff team of my church at a church leaders' conference hosted by New Wine Network.

I was at a pivotal time in my ministry. I'd served the church for 7 years as an associate pastor and I'd become lethargic in my vision. The week before the conference I'd had one of the worst meetings of my life with our senior pastor Dave who probed me on *why I was doing what I was doing*. I felt utterly crushed and empty. This was the closest I'd ever come to giving up on ministry. I almost didn't go to the conference as I felt the raw wounds from my meeting with Dave. We talked and prayed, and I knew deep down that Dave's words were underpinned by love—but I still felt terrible. Dave convinced me to go—it was something we'd planned all year and he didn't want me to miss out.

This conference was the first time I heard Bill Johnson speak. Bill has since become a hero of mine. His wisdom and revelation has impacted and shaped my life and thinking in so many ways.

As the conference progressed I had the feeling that I'd been set up by God. I could sense that God wanted me in this 'empty' place so that He could fill me right up to the brim

---

102 A.W. Tozer, Gems from Tozer: Selections from the Writings of A.W. Tozer

and overflowing.

The final evening of the conference came and I knew I had a choice—that God was going to pour His Spirit out on me but also that, to receive Him, I needed to hand everything over. I'd reached a point where I was past every bit of human pride that I was carrying. I just said in my heart *God do what you want with me. I don't care what people think anymore. It's you or nothing.*

The Spirit worked on me in different ways that night. Some were visible, some were unseen. I felt the weight of His presence so strongly that I could hardly walk. I laughed so much I could sense healing taking place. That night changed my ministry forever. His outpouring positioned me, it realigned me, refreshed me and empowered me.

It was shortly after this time that I became the prophetic pastor of the Church. This was such a fruitful time of ministry where I was able to grow a healthy prophetic ministry in the church for many years before leaving to emigrate to the U.S.

Why the Spirit does this when he does remains a mystery. When I reflect on life, I know that those times when the Spirit has poured joy over me have been intelligently designed by God to give me every chance to succeed in life and ministry. I'm sure when we look back on our lives, we will see these moments in their full significance.

Life to the Full: *Purpose*

> *True happiness... is not attained through self-gratification, but through fidelity to a worthy purpose.*[103]

Every person needs to know their purpose. Life without purpose is incomplete because – at the core of our being – we need to know that we're here for a reason. One's purpose is rarely a straight path. There can be many routes to take and roles to play in a lifetime. A popular belief is that we discover our purpose at a certain age, but this simply isn't the case. Instead, purpose is an ever evolving road on which we walk. There can be many crossroads, fast lanes and back-roads along the way. We need God to be our ever-present guide if we are to truly seize our purposes in life.

The Word and the Spirit continually serve to help us stay on the right path. They're passionate about seeing our purposes revealed to us and fulfilled.

The Word Lights the Way

There's nothing worse than navigating in the dark. Even if you have a map it can go wrong. When Titus was about six months old we decided to go on a little family retreat. We were to stay in a friend's holiday home in Cornwall, England. We decided to leave Bristol around 6pm so that Titus would sleep most of the trip.

103 Helen Keller

The journey took longer than we expected and we arrived in the area at around 11 at night. It was deep Cornish countryside; the roads small and narrow, twisted and turned. There was very little light. Unfortunately for us, two things exacerbated the situation; Titus woke up screaming and heavy rain started. Our stress levels skyrocketed when we could barely see through the intense night rain while Titus screamed from the back seat. We had the directions written down from our friend, but it seemed like the roads just didn't exist and we felt as though we were driving in circles.

Midnight arrived with little change, and while lost in the forest, we reluctantly phoned our friends for directions. Thankfully they were awake, and being the kindest of people, talked us through the journey until we eventually found the house.

The following morning we took a drive around and realized how easy the drive was in daylight but how cunningly hidden it could be in the darkness.

The Bible tells us that one of the many roles the Word plays in our lives is being light to our path.

> *Your word is a lamp to my feet, and a light for my path.*[104]

When it comes to our purpose, God's Word literally helps us see where we are going. There will be moments in life where our purpose seems foggy, where we feel like we're moving

---

104 Psalms 119:105 NIV

blindly through the dark. It's especially these times that we need God's Word because it acts as a light illuminating the way forward.

I've experienced this first-hand. I've had long stretches of time where I've clearly known where I'm headed. I'm a visionary by nature, so seeing ahead is what I do. It's usually what I'm good at. But in 2012 we made to bold move to emigrate from the UK to the U.S. Chris, my husband is originally from California—he'd spent the previous 7 years married to me in the UK and we both sensed that God wanted to replant us. It was such a difficult decision for me. My family and friends were firmly rooted in Bristol and I was thriving in my role as the prophetic pastor at Woodlands Church.

As we ventured out, we knew little of spiritual transition—never before had I experienced this type of U-turn in my journey of 'purpose'. During the first couple years it was like walking through fog—such a frustrating experience for a visionary. I was unable to 'see' what was next for me. The need to know the importance of God's Word had never been stronger in my life. It didn't get rid of the fog, but it did light up my path and affirmed that I was indeed heading in the right direction.

There were many times during those two years where God's prophetic Word just kept me on track, and just as many when I questioned whether we'd made the right decision. But God kept assuring me that this was part of my journey. A transition across a desert that would lead to somewhere good. He kept assuring me that – even in this arid environment – He was doing a work that was shaping me for what was to come.

I remember one morning getting a Facebook message from a lady that I'd known in my home church. She said that she'd had a number of dreams about me and asked if it was okay to share. Here's part of what she wrote;

> *Last night I had another dream where God was audibly telling me to tell you that you were to wait patiently for him and that he is never late neither is he ever early as his timing is perfect. I'm not sure if this means anything to you right now but as I've never heard directly the voice of God before in a dream I felt I should pass this on. Sorry you got this in dribs and drabs. Bless you! Your children always look gorgeous.*
>
> *Love, Joan x*

For me this was such a blessing. Firstly, the fact that God spoke to someone halfway across the World just to give me a message simply blew my mind. Secondly, this was so accurate and timely. I had been wavering and contemplating taking a different direction than what God had firmly placed on my heart. I was in a place of "nothing's happening" and was getting very bored by it. I was tempted to make stuff happen my own, but here in God's grace, He interjected with His Word. He shone His light once again on my journey and reassured me that He had this in His hands.

God's Word Invests in Us

One of my favorite TV shows is *Shark Tank* (or *Dragon's Den* for the UK). For those of you who've never watched it, it's a show where a panel of four multi-billionaire's personalities sit and listen to people's pitches for inventions and business ideas. The entrepreneur hopefuls are asking for an investment of money, and in return are willing to give away a share of their business. It's a show full of drama. You get to see some amazing creative ideas. You witness how *not* to do a sales pitch. You see the joy hit people when someone wants to invest in them, and you see grown men and women weep when no one will invest in their dreams.

A staggering truth revealed in the Bible is that God's Word invests in us. It teaches us that God sends forth His Word into our lives, and it's value is so high that it won't return to Him until it brings about the very purpose for which it was sent.

Here we see a passage in Isaiah that likens the Word to rain and snow. It's an incredible statement of the type of wealth that the Word is and the type of investor God is to us:

> *As the rain and the snow*
> *come down from heaven,*
> *and do not return to it*
> *without watering the earth*
> *and making it bud and flourish,*
> *so that it yields seed for the sower and bread for the eater,*
> *so is my word that goes out from my mouth:*
> *It will not return to me empty,*
> *but will accomplish what I desire*
> *and achieve the purpose for which I sent it.*[105]

---

105   Isaiah 55:10-11 NIV

Not only does the Word give us clarity of where we need to go and what we need to avoid, but it's also the currency of the biggest investor of the universe – Father God – whose passion is to infuse his currency into our dreams and passions so that they thrive within us.

The Spirit Guides Us

One of the great truths about the Holy Spirit is that He's our companion. It's so reassuring to me that we don't have to do this pilgrimage alone. He's the best companion anyone could wish for because He carries all knowledge, all truth and all wisdom in His being. God's Spirit walks with us, and He's not silent because He's also our guide.

The gospel of John describes Him like this:

> *But when he, the Spirit of truth, comes, he will guide you into all the truth. He will not speak on his own; he will speak only what he hears, and he will tell you what is yet to come.*[106]

This knowledge should make us feel very confident. God Himself is helping us get to where we should be and become who we need to be.

A guide – in human terms – is someone who has prior experience of the journey. They're hired to give expert knowledge of what to expect and advice on where to go.

---

106   John 16:13 NIV

The Holy Spirit Speaks

One of the ways that the Spirit guides us is through speaking to us. He will continually interject with His advice as we pursue our purpose. This advice involves encouraging us, giving us understanding, directing us and even warning us of obstacles or dead ends in our path.

It's important to know the spectrum of advice that He imparts. Some people believe, for example, that the Spirit will always give direction, and then they find themselves never moving forward for lack of a Word from the Spirit. This comes from a misunderstanding of the Spirit's role to us. Directing us is only one part of His role as guide. There may be many parts of our journey where the Holy Spirit, in His wisdom, doesn't direct us but instead encourages us or gives us understanding of the journey we're on.

It's vital therefore that we ask the right questions of the Spirit when we are seeking to fulfill our purpose.

The Spirit speaks all the time in many different ways. I know many people count themselves out from hearing from Him because of a plethora of limited teaching on how He speaks.

One of the things I loved to do when I teach on the prophetic gift is to really unpack how God speaks today through His Spirit. I usually start with a group whom 80% don't believe they hear from God and end up with the whole group beaming because they finally realize that *maybe, just maybe,* God speaks to them too.

Scripture, creation, dreams, visions, circumstances, small still voice, audible voice, songs and movies are just some of the ways God speaks and gets our attention. He speaks to us individually and also uses others to share His words with us.

As a guide, there *are* times He brings direction. I've witnessed some amazing moments where the Spirit brought Words into people's lives and how these Words have given such clear direction.

One of these stories is the story of Debbie. Debbie was a regularly involved member of our church. As part of my work to grow the prophetic ministry in the church, I'd set up monthly 'prophecy clinics'—slots people could book into and get a small trained team to prophesy over them. Overall, this ministry was a great success and asset to the church. The team got to practice and exercise their gift in a safe setting and the people who came often got incredibly blessed by the affirming Words of the Father. The prophecy clinics are still being run today by an incredible leadership team. Debbie booked herself into one of these slots over 6 years ago and God spoke in a way that changed her life. I wrote to her recently and asked her if she'd write up the account for this book. Here's her story:

> *I was in a job that I didn't feel passionate about. I was working as a teacher in a Secondary School teaching German and I felt like there must be more to life than this. At the same time, I was living in one of the church community houses and we had undergone recent change, with people from the community getting married. A new member of the community started to stir me up out of my*

comfort zone and challenged me about what my passions were and what I was living for. I had become lukewarm in my relationship with God and had become a consumer christian but at the same time sensed a change coming in my life but didn't know what this could look like.

At the beginning of every year, my church has a week of prayer and fasting and an opportunity to get a prophetic team to listen to God with and for you. I decided to sign up for one of these slots and little did I realize the significance it would have.

I sat in a group of around four people who were dedicated to listening to God for my life. None of them particularly knew what was going on with me – which was great because I knew that if God spoke it would be easy to identify. There were many words given but what sticks out now looking back was a prophetic word Ruth had of two things: a house and a crossroads both of which had a question mark over them. Ruth went onto talk about the crossroad situation and making a decision for God. She said she sensed that if I went with what God had, it would result in unprecedented growth in my walk with Him and adventure.

Berlin had been on my heart for a long time. Having studied German and European Studies at University, I'd always had a niggling dream to plant christian communities in the former East of Germany, previously under communism, in order to spread the good news about Jesus. But I'd never really taken this seriously.

By the end of that day, I'd booked flights to visit Berlin with a view to spending time in the 24-7 prayer community near Leipzig. They had previously told me I could come and visit any time I wanted. The 24-7 prayer community got back to me saying, yes come whenever you want, just not the week you have booked.

I was flummoxed - it was strange to have flights booked and not have any specific itinerary. I didn't know any christians in Berlin, so I emailed all my contacts around Germany and was put in contact with a British Couple, who'd moved to Berlin and were wanting to start a missions school. I then realized that there was a Christian conference taking place in Berlin during my visit too. I booked into the conference to see if I could network with people. It wasn't what I initially thought I'd be doing during my visit but God has a way of orchestrating the right things to do in the right time.

Over the course of my visit to Berlin one thing remained crystal clear - I knew God was calling me there.

When I returned to Bristol I handed in my notice at work and signed up to do the missions year that the British Couple were organizing. It was a fantastic year and I have since joined the vineyard church-planting team, where we have a vision to plant christian communities in all 96 districts of Berlin. In order to get by financially, I have been working part-time in a kindergarten teaching English in East Berlin.

I've now been in Berlin for 6 and a half years and been involved in various ministries here, including Teen Challenge and the BURN (24 hour worship). This week,

> *I'm launching my first community plant! God is good!*

This is such a fantastic story of how the Holy Spirit speaks in a way to propel purpose. For Debbie, she was discontent because she wasn't living this life to the full that Jesus had promised. But the Spirit worked in such a marvelous way—guiding her into the place where she could thrive and know that she is living out everything that God has purposed for her life.

Knowing and *living out our purpose* is such a fundamental part of life to the full. The Word and the Spirit are our active agents, fully committed to seeing each one of our lives' life-purpose come to fruition.

Life to the Full: *Power*

> *All giants have been weak men who did great things for God because they reckoned on His power and presence to be with them.*[107]

God wants us to be powerful. We need to be powerful because we are called to minister the kingdom of God to people, cities and nations all over the world. There are just too many desperate situations that require God's people to intervene with His power.

We were created to be powerful—being made in God's image, He gave us authority to rule over the world. As sin entered

---

107   Hudson Taylor

the world it corrupted power like everything else it touched. Since then we've witnessed the atrocities of abused power, but as we accept Jesus and walk into full redemption, we realize that we are meant to be powerful people and that the reality of receiving power from God is firmly on the table.

The church is meant to be full of powerful people administering God's kingdom on earth as it is in heaven.

Power is another gift of life that brings fullness and completion when it's grounded in love. It's a benefit that allows us to impact the world around us, to stand up to the evils that exist and tear them down. Power gives us the ability to establish new creative ways of living.

The Word and the Spirit give power to those who are devoted to Jesus. This power is not of human origin, but heavenly. It's the same power that blasted the stone away from the grave where Jesus body lay, the same power that Jesus healed multitudes, the same power that raised Lazarus from the dead, the same power that forgave the paraplegics of their sins. This is the power of God for which the disciples were told to wait, because with it they were destined to change the world.

The Spirit Anoints us with Power

The most famous demonstration of people being anointed with the Spirit's power is the story of how the Holy Spirit descended upon the 120 disciples at Pentecost.

Right before Jesus ascended to heaven, He told the disciples to not leave Jerusalem, but to wait for the gift of The Holy

Spirit which was the Father's promise:

> *But you will receive power when the Holy Spirit comes on you; and you will be my witnesses in Jerusalem, and in all Judea and Samaria, and to the ends of the earth.*[108]

They gathered together, hidden, waiting and praying, and then very dramatically the Holy Spirit came:

> *When the Day of Pentecost had fully come, they were all with one accord in one place. And suddenly there came a sound from heaven, as of a rushing mighty wind, and it filled the whole house where they were sitting. Then there appeared to them divided tongues, as of fire, and one sat upon each of them. And they were all filled with the Holy Spirit and began to speak with other tongues, as the Spirit gave them utterance.*[109]

It was this gift of the Spirit Himself that empowered this fearful group of believers to become disciples that took on the world.

The consequence of this was outstanding. These people were filled with supernatural boldness and spoke different languages. Immediately the fruit of this power is evident as Peter's infamous anointed speech sees about three thousand of the crowd believe in Jesus that day, and it didn't stop there.

---

108   Acts 1:8 NIV
109   Acts 2:1-4 NKJV

We see the accounts of how the disciples taught new believers to receive the Spirit. Receiving the power of the Holy Spirit was taught as a fundamental part of following Christ.

Today the Holy Spirit's power is available to every believer just like it was in New Testament times. In my experience, Christians have mixed reactions about the power of God. I guess it's the same as Earthly power—we know it has benefits but we also know it can be abused.

The fact that the power of the Spirit is a gift from the Father, though, should make us more comfortable. We certainly need to embrace wisdom and understanding and learn how to use the power of God, but we owe it to a world in need of breakthrough to receive and use that power.

In my own journey of receiving the Spirit's power I've had many ups and downs. I've had seasons of eagerly desiring God's power for breakthrough, often very tunnel visioned. I've had times where I've been disillusioned with it because I've been convinced that other truths need to balance it out. But then I come back to it again with a more long-term view; knowing that it's ultimately a great gift from God but equally knowing it needs grounding and instruction.

> *We must have a spirit of power towards the enemy, a spirit of love towards men, and a spirit of self-control towards ourselves.*[110]

---

110 Watchman Nee, The Normalcy of the Spirit

Receiving the Spirit's power is a huge part of the Christians life to the full. It ignites us to fulfill what God has commissioned us to do.

The Power of the Gospel

> *For I am not ashamed of the gospel, because it is the power of God that brings salvation to everyone who believes: first to the Jew, then to the Gentile.*[111]

The good news of Christ is the power of God that brings salvation. Jesus' life, His death and resurrection, the story of the Word made flesh is potently powerful. We mustn't forget this as Christians. Sometimes our churches are so full of our own ideas or programs that it's easy for us to rely on our own persuasive words and actions, forgetting the sheer power of the gospel preached.

I'm sure God likes our efforts (at least some of the time). I'm sure He loves our creativity with all the multimedia presentations. But the story of Jesus, all on it's own, has the power to save the most depraved human being from the clutches of sin.

One of the most striking conversion stories in the Bible is that of Saul of Tarsus—a persecutor of Christians who was struck blind by the power of Jesus on His way to Damascus:

> *As he journeyed he came near Damascus, and suddenly a*

---

[111] Romans 1:16 NIV

> *light shone around him from heaven. Then he fell to the ground, and heard a voice saying to him, "Saul, Saul, why are you persecuting Me?" And he said, "Who are You, Lord?" Then the Lord said, "I am Jesus, whom you are persecuting. It is hard for you to kick against the goads." So he, trembling and astonished, said, "Lord, what do You want me to do?" Then the Lord said to him, "Arise and go into the city, and you will be told what you must do."* [112]

Saul experienced first-hand the power of the gospel of Jesus Christ. It shook him to his core and turned his life around. Jesus – the Word made flesh – is power. If we're ever feeling a lack of power to minister or witness or simply live our lives, it's wise to meditate on His life. As we do so, the Word will infuse us with dynamism.

God's Word is a Powerful Weapon

> *For the word of God is living and powerful, and sharper than any two-edged sword, piercing even to the division of soul and spirit, and of joints and marrow, and is a discerner of the thoughts and intents of the heart.* [113]

The Spirit anoints us with power and the Word is a powerful weapon. We've already seen how the Bible describes the Word as a sword, a hammer and fire. These analogies all lend themselves to displaying the truth that the Word of God becomes a powerful instrument that we can use to bring breakthrough.

---

112 Acts 9:1-19 NKJV
113 Hebrews 4:12 NKJV

I hope this chapter has inspired you to see how important the Word and the Spirit are in our lives as Christians. If you're passionate about Christ's church, I hope these words have ignited a desire in you to pursue the Word and the Spirit in your church setting. The benefits for us in embracing the Word and the Spirit far outweigh any reasons we could have in positioning ourselves in one at the expense of the other.

The following final two chapters are an invitation to dive in deep. They're not for those who wish to remain on the sidelines. But instead, they will call you into a passionate life where the Word and the Spirit are put center-stage.

6
passion for the word

> *One person with passion is better than forty people merely interested.* [114]

It's one thing being agreeable that the Word is important in our Christian journey, it's quite another to be passionate about it. I'm a people watcher, I love to observe people from a distance, especially Christians. There have been several times in my life where I've observed a Christian and their passion has been so authentic and compelling that it's made me question what they've got that I haven't.

One of the first times this happened to me was when I heard Jackie Pullinger speak at a conference. It was a small group of 30-40 people. As she spoke, I witnessed a compelling love in her for Jesus that I'd never seen before. Her keynote speech was nothing spectacular. I'd already heard the amazing stories from her book *Chasing the Dragon*. She wasn't particularly humorous or even charismatic in her presentation. Yet she

---

114 E. M. Forster

stood in front of me and as she spoke, she spoke from a deep well of love that was rare. Her eyes sparkled with a secret and I left knowing that she had something that I didn't. I promised myself that day that I would spend my lifetime getting the same passion for Jesus as she had. It reminded me of the parable that Jesus told about the merchant who sold everything he had to get the one pearl [115]. Gaining a passion does cost us, but it's worth is of immeasurable value.

In this chapter I want to invite you on a journey of developing a passion for the Word. I want us to be known not only as people of the Word, but as people who are insanely passionate about the Word. Passion is a driving force that evolves from a deep love. It takes us beyond the normal and empowers us to live extraordinary lives. I believe God is wanting to evoke a passion for both the Word and the Spirit in His church today. So let's look at these three aspects of the Word – Scripture, Jesus and Prophecy – and wrestle with where our passion is and how we can grow it.

A Passion for Scripture

> *To candid, reasonable men, I am not afraid to lay open what have been the inmost thoughts of my heart. I have thought, I am a creature of a day, passing through life as an arrow through the air. I am a spirit come from God, and returning to God: just hovering over the great gulf; till, a few moments hence, I am no more seen; I drop into an unchangeable eternity! I want to know one thing,—the way*

---

115 Matthew 13:45

to heaven; how to land safe on that happy shore. God himself has condescended to teach me the way. For this very end He came from heaven. He hath written it down in a book. O give me that book! At any price, give me the book of God! [116]

John Wesley was a man who was passionate about scripture. How many Christians do you know who – in a Bible Study or at the coffee bar at church – shake their fist and say *"O give me that book! At any price, give me the book of God!"* It's a passionate plea, one we very rarely glimpse today. In fact, many Christians barely survive the sometimes mundane task of their daily reading. I am always struck when I read these types of quotes or when I witness raw passion for scripture. Not long ago a video was posted on Youtube of a group of Chinese students receiving Bibles for the first time. Tears and joy ensued. It was a scene that would make the average western Christian stop and reflect about their own feelings for this book.

In my own life I have been fortunate enough to be exposed to two very dear friends and colleagues who simply love scripture. Pam Scott-Cook has been in senior leadership of my home church for many years she is one of the warmest, joy-filled (and downright hilarious) people I know. Clare Thompson, another senior leader whose deep thinking, great preaching and counsel impacts many. I served on our staff team with both these ladies for many years.

As a staff team we would meet every Monday to review and

---

[116] Henry Craik, ed. English Prose. 1916, Vol. IV. Eighteenth Century, A Man of One Book By John Wesley (1703–1791)

plan the various departments and activities of church life, but before all of the business, someone would always bring a devotional. I'm writing this with fond memories and a smile on my face because whenever either of these ladies would take a turn to lead the devotional, they would simply gush scripture. They would talk about a verse as if it were a piece of fine jewelry and swoon over how this or that scripture had impacted them. I would sit there sipping my coffee, barely awake, wondering what on Earth they had been smoking. At the time I intellectually appreciated scripture, but it hadn't grabbed my heart like it obviously had with Pam and Clare. I'm so glad I got to see this because it made me hungry for more.

How to Fall in Love with Scripture

Psalm 1 gives some compelling instruction about how we should treat scripture and it's benefits:

> *Blessed is the one*
> *who does not walk in step with the wicked*
> *or stand in the way that sinners take*
> *or sit in the company of mockers,*
> *but whose delight is in the law of the Lord,*
> *and who meditates on his law day and night.*
> *That person is like a tree planted by streams of water,*
> *which yields its fruit in season*
> *and whose leaf does not wither—*
> *whatever they do prospers.*[117]

---

117 Psalm 1:1-3 NIV

Here the word 'law' is referring to scripture, or the 'logos' Word. *The Message* version of the Bible puts it like this:

> *How well God must like you— you don't hang out at Sin Saloon, you don't slink along Dead-End Road, you don't go to Smart-Mouth College. Instead you thrill to God's Word, you chew on Scripture day and night. You're a tree replanted in Eden, bearing fresh fruit every month. Never dropping a leaf, always in blossom.*

At the beginning of this famous psalm there's a teaching about the way we feel and handle scripture, and how beneficial it is when we do it well. It doesn't say 'blessed are those who manage to do a bible reading every morning', it says that the ones who are blessed (happy) are the ones who 'delight' or are 'thrilled by' God's word. This brings the way we treat scripture to a different level.

Let me ask you some questions:

> *How do you fall in love with scripture?*

> *How do you get to a place where you are delighting in and thrilled by His written Word?*

> *Is it a personality thing?*

> *Do some people naturally love it more than others, or is there more to it than that?*

After witnessing the genuine affection for scripture in my

friends Pam and Clare, and after reading quotes such as the likes of John Wesley, and when I reflect on how my own grandmother cherished scripture—these are the questions that have been part of my journey.

I believe this psalm sets a standard to be passionate about scripture. It's an offer to all regardless of age, sex, personality or race. The promise of *being like a tree planted by streams of water* is not only for a select few who enjoy literature, but is meant to be something that every ordinary Christian can attain. If this is true, the big question is *how do we get there?*

The Psalms contain a wealth of knowledge and understanding. There are lots of little treasures in them that we need to search out. If we're interested in falling in love with scripture, we need to take a closer look at Psalm 1—the wisdom that's available is key for us to move forward.

Let's look at Psalm 1, verse 2:

> *but whose delight is in the law of the Lord, and who meditates on his law day and night.*

The two phrases that are crucial for us to unpack are 'meditates on' and 'day and night'. These two phrases say something striking about the way we're supposed to approach scripture. When they are twinned like this they give a double punch of wisdom.

Firstly, let's look at the phrase 'mediates on'. The word *meditate* suggests something more than a once-off read of scripture. It refers to what happens during and after that scripture is read.

Just to get us to fully appreciate the word *meditate*, here are some of it's synonyms:

> *mull over, ponder, reflect upon, weigh, have in mind, puzzle over, brood over, dream, entertain idea, think deeply*

This is what we are meant to do with scripture. All of these synonyms show an activity that in very nature takes time—certainly more time than most people's dedicated slot for reading their Bible.

My most overt experience of this is when I've been preparing to preach. In fact, I've come to realize that one of the reasons I love preaching is that it forces me into the activity of meditating on God's Word. It's an incredibly stimulating experience. Having a passage to 'wrestle with' over a week or so enables you to go deep, gain unique perspective and feel like you've found the treasure of God. This is something Psalm 1 is advising us to do every time we read scripture—not only when we're preaching or are looking for something to say.

The Psalm then pushes the teaching even further with this second phrase 'day and night'. *Day and night* lends itself to meaning *continuously—all the hours of life itself.* It's suggesting that scripture isn't just something we read, but it's something we wear, something we carry, something that rests on us. It becomes part of us. As we carry it around, we meditate upon it or chew on it until it brings forth its fruit.

Learning to meditate on scripture day and night has to have a starting point. The starting point is to carve out time daily to read the Bible. This is something we do in order to effect our whole day - there's a certain level of discipline or habit around it. It's an activity that's like getting dressed each day and picking out which clothes to wear. What we're essentially doing as we open our Bibles and read a passage is *choosing what scripture to put on that day*.

As we learn to do this, we'll find that scripture becomes far more than a daily duty. These writings of history, wisdom, prose and prophecy that have been Spirit-breathed will become part of us. They will plant us by those streams of living water, bringing us into a place of prosperity.

Discovering your Personal History with Scripture

We need to know the importance of our relationship with scripture. *Personal relationship with scripture?* Yes—you heard me right. I cannot think of an area in my life that I'm passionate about that hasn't impacted me personally. There's plenty of stuff I respect out there, but I get passionate about people/ideas/things when they are in my life and affecting me. With scripture – unless we have or build a personal history with it – we'll find it will be hard to delight in it. Sometimes it's as simple as recognizing that we do have a personal history with scripture and that's enough to spark a flame.

So what does a personal history with scripture look like? Generally speaking it's when passages or verses or even whole books have been significantly attached to your life's moments; when you became a Christian, when you got married, when you went through a trial, when you got healed, when you needed hope. All of these and more. Significant moments and seasons of life where scripture has been there in a powerful way.

For me, when I think of my personal history with scripture, I envision it as a wall of fame where my scriptures stand tall. I recognize the different types of scripture and what they've achieved for me. Check out my wall of fame, these are some examples of the type of scriptures that have impacted me.

My Wall of Fame

1. Heroes of War

These are scriptures that have brought me victory. I've been given them by God at certain times of my life where I've struggled and they've brought me through. They have done battle with me.

> *And the peace of God, which transcends all understanding, will guard your hearts and your minds in Christ Jesus.*[118]

This verse helped bring me victory over fear. I remember a particular season of my life where fear gripped my heart in ungodly way and I pinned this scripture up everywhere in my house. I would read it five or six times a day. I just knew it had power to bring me victory and freedom—and it did!

There's a strong emotional connection with scripture that's fought a battle with you. They're like wartime heroes that you applaud and celebrate.

---

[118] Philippians 4:7 NIV

2. Faithful Companions

These scriptures are the ones that have been a constant part of my journey. They're the scriptures that have been part of the monumental times of my life. God uses them again and again to remind me of my journey and encourage faith.

One such scripture for me are the verses in Hebrews about faith:

> *Now faith is confidence in what we hope for and assurance about what we do not see. This is what the ancients were commended for.*[119]

This scripture first impacted me when I was a new Christian. I had given my life to God and decided that I should move from Cardiff to Bristol. I distinctly remember a weekend when I went to Bristol looking for work so that I could plan my move. It was such a demoralizing time which seemed that every door of opportunity was shut. I remember sinking down in my sofa with a cup of tea and my Bible and I opened it to Hebrews 11. As I read this famous chapter about faith, the Holy Spirit was stirring my spirit. I read about these amazing heroes of faith and decided that *if God wanted me in Bristol, I didn't need any reassurances.* That day I gave my notice at my job in Cardiff and scheduled to move to Bristol within the month. The rest is history. A great 13 years in a city I love!

Since then, this scripture has come to me at times when

---

119   Hebrews 11:1-2 NIV

I'm faltering in faith. In times where I've lost perspective, this scripture always seems to pop up. Whenever I see this scripture I have strong recollection of that pivotal moment in my early Christian life and something happens in my spirit. It's like I'm anchored, reassured and inspired once more to fight the good fight of faith.

3. Pools of Refreshment

These are scriptures that I find myself going back to when I know my Spirit needs refreshing. I find that their effect on me is like going for a swim on a hot sunny day. They're places I can dive into and allow my spirit to soak in His goodness. They're usually scriptures that declare promises, truth and the sheer goodness of God.

I have so many of these scriptures that refresh my spirit. One significant one for me is Psalm 84:

> *How lovely is your dwelling place,*
> *Lord Almighty!*
> *My soul yearns, even faints,*
> *for the courts of the Lord;*
> *my heart and my flesh cry out*
> *for the living God.*
> *Even the sparrow has found a home,*
> *and the swallow a nest for herself,*
> *where she may have her young—*
> *a place near your altar,*
> *Lord Almighty, my King and my God.*
> *Blessed are those who dwell in your house;*
> *they are ever praising you.*

Blessed are those whose strength is in you,
whose hearts are set on pilgrimage.
As they pass through the Valley of Baka,
they make it a place of springs;
the autumn rains also cover it with pools.
They go from strength to strength,
till each appears before God in Zion.
Hear my prayer, Lord God Almighty;
listen to me, God of Jacob.
Look on our shield,[e] O God;
look with favor on your anointed one.
Better is one day in your courts
than a thousand elsewhere;
I would rather be a doorkeeper in the house of my God
than dwell in the tents of the wicked.
For the Lord God is a sun and shield;
the Lord bestows favor and honor;
no good thing does he withhold
from those whose walk is blameless.
Lord Almighty, blessed is the one who trusts in you.[120]

This Psalm is always good for me if I'm feeling weary. It has a way of uplifting my soul.

4. Fine Dining Rooms of Revelation

There are scriptures that I go to when I'm spiritually hungry. They are places where I know I can chew on some spiritual meat. They're passages that have layers of meaning. Verses that

120   NIV

contain a degree of mystery. These aren't necessarily places of reassurance, but instead ports of voyage and discovery. They keep me growing. They stimulate me intellectually. They allow me to question, and in doing so, gain wisdom and understanding.

I'm sure some of you have experienced what it's like to be stuck in a book of the Bible for a while, wrestling with it's meaning and impressed with it's unfolding layers of revelation. One of my favorite books in the Bible for this is Ephesians. There have been many seasons in my life where I've spent months in this book, unpacking the topics raised by Paul.

✦

These are just some examples from my life to get you thinking about your own personal history with Scripture. Obviously yours will be different from mine, but point is that you do have or can make a history with scripture. Taking the time to recognize you have one is an essential part of gaining a growing passion for it.

Take some time to reflect. Maybe ask yourself some of these questions;

What scriptures have brought me through a trial?

Are there any scriptures that I claim as my own?

What scriptures get my thinking?

What scriptures bring me comfort?

A Passion for the Gospel of Jesus

Gaining a passion for the Word involves growing a passion for the gospel of Jesus Christ. The gospel is the 'good news' of Jesus—His life, death and resurrection and what that means for us today. As we've learned, Jesus is God's Word made flesh. He became God with us, so that we might fully know the goodness of God and have a way to become adopted into God's family.

The good news of Jesus is God's most dynamic piece of revelation to us. It stunned the heavenly realms and shook the kingdom of darkness to its core. God not only reached out to mankind and identified with every part of life, but He also masterfully executed a plan. A plan that redeemed what had been stolen and saved what was lost. A plan that healed the broken, cleansed the stain of sin and most importantly, gave people of every race a way back into relationship with Him, the Father of the Universe.

> *Jesus answered, "I am the way and the truth and the life. No one comes to the Father except through me."*[121]

---

121   John 14:6 NIV

A Gift that Changes your Life Forever

The Word made flesh is the greatest gift to humanity that God could give—His own begotten son sent to live among us, identify with us, die for us and conquer death's power over us. Jesus embodies the greatest gift of love we've ever known. When a person encounters the gift of this gospel it changes their life forever.

Perhaps one of the most famous hymns of all time is John Newton's 'Amazing grace'. Like so many others, I love this old hymn because it encapsulates that overwhelming sense of wonder when a person first encounters the true revelation of the life of Jesus.

> *Amazing grace! (how sweet the sound)*
>   *That sav'd a wretch like me!*
> *I once was lost, but now am found,*
>   *Was blind, but now I see.*
>
> *'Twas grace that taught my heart to fear,*
>   *And grace my fears reliev'd;*
> *How precious did that grace appear*
>   *The hour I first believ'd!* [122]

---

[122] lyricstranslate.com, Amazing Grace (original version), John Newton 1779

The Moment you First Believed

We will all have different stories and approaches to understanding and embracing Jesus. For those of you that have given your lives to Jesus, do you remember that first moment you believed? It's good to reminisce.

I love hearing the stories of salvation; where the truth of the gospel penetrates a person's soul, where the implications of what Christ achieved start to sink in. For John Newton, this revelation was so stark it was as if he was blind but then was able to see.

Few of us will get the full meaning of the cross in those early moments. I certainly didn't—for me it was more like a sure clarity came upon me that seized my very by being. I knew that I knew that Jesus was for real, and I knew that it was good news for me. I didn't know all the ins and outs, but I knew enough to sense that He would change my life.

There's always a journey up to that point—the point when we realize that Jesus will change our life forever. For some it's many years of pursued learning, a *gaining* so to speak, of knowledge about Jesus. For others it can be a momentary journey where this revelation hits in a way that is indisputable. And then there are many other types of journeys in-between. But there always comes a point of realization that we've just received the gift of a lifetime, and when that happens, a passion floods our hearts like nothing we've experienced before.

Passion for Jesus will only ever really come when we discover that the gift of Jesus is such good news. *Great* news. The best news ever. We get that first dose of passion for the gospel when we encounter it for ourselves. Passion for the gospel always starts with us and our own discovery of it.

A Gift that Keeps on Giving

Whatever passion you have at the beginning of your journey, and whichever way you express it, it's essential to understand that it's a seed in you that can and will grow. It's not a once-off deposit, but instead the beginning of a love that will deepen, mature and evolve into a life laid down for Christ over the course of a lifetime.

The gift of salvation that Jesus gives is ever-unfolding. We continually discover it's value and it's impact for our lives. There are layers upon layers of it's meaning and truth. Part of gaining a passion for the gospel of Jesus is understanding that passion for it grows as we experience its effects upon our lives. It's a gift that keeps on giving. As we live out our days through the many seasons that are thrown our way, the revelation continues to unfold of this glorious gift of Jesus' sacrifice.

There will continue to be many times in our lives where the revelation of the life of Jesus sinks deeper and fresh doses of passion for it are unleashed. It's because this gift has several different facets—it can take an entire lifetime to understand the richness of just one. Grace, redemption, freedom, adoption, justification and healing are just some of the many aspects of the gospel of Jesus. As we navigate our life through our successes, failures, pain, suffering, joy and life, our inner being absorbs more and more truth about these things.

I want us to take a look at how some significant life events can shape and fuel our passion for Jesus.

Our Failings

None of us set out in life to fail, and yet we all do. Some of us fail big and some of us fail in the less noticeable things. It's through grace that God uses our failings to grow our passion for Him. In fact, it's often those heart-sinking failures that are actually opportunities where God can stir a fire in our heart that was never there before.

Jesus shares this wisdom with His disciples after their disdain is voiced for the woman who anointed Jesus feet with oil.

> *For this reason I say to you, her sins, which are many, have been forgiven, for she loved much; but he who is forgiven little, loves little.*[123]

The times of our lives when we mess up and come back to God looking for His forgiveness are actually precious moments where we taste new revelations of His grace—and that knowledge of grace stirs the waters of gratitude, love and passion like nothing else.

---

123   Luke 7:47 NASB

The life of the apostle Peter is a case study of this. If there was ever a charismatically passionate follower of Jesus it was this ruddy fisherman. And yet, of all Jesus' disciples, Peter had one of the most public epic fails. After Jesus is arrested, Peter denies his knowledge of Jesus three times, even though previously he'd boasted of his intention to lay down his life for his Lord. Peter couldn't follow through on his professed passion for Jesus. His words and his actions weren't aligned in this moment of time.

Yet in this miserable place of failure, the risen Jesus comes to Peter and pours out grace. Not only does He allow Peter to redeem himself by professing his love for Jesus three times, but He also entrusts the building the Church to Peter. This is insanity by human standards. Promotion, in the world's eyes, doesn't go to those who screw up. But here Jesus models the way of heaven, where failure becomes a secret garden of grace where seeds of promotion are planted.

As we fail and come back to Jesus, we only realize even more how undeserving we are. In these humble moments where we know we don't deserve anything, Jesus comes to us forgives us and offers us the positions of kings. It's during these times, where our soul is in awe of the mysteries of grace and sings out *How can this be?* that we truly grow in passion for Him.

Creation

Observing life unfolding can be one of the most profound spiritual teaching grounds. Jesus always anchored His teaching and revelation in analogies that His disciples could grasp, and it's here in life itself that we can attain depths of knowledge and understanding of this gospel of Jesus. As our knowledge and understanding grows, so too will our passion.

New parents find a deeper understanding of the Father's love as they themselves enter a phase of life where sacrificial love becomes a hallmark. They can identify with certain aspects of the gospel more now than before. I've seen people have their faith in Jesus renewed as they've become parents, as the striking correlation of parental emotions brings clarity's due weight to the gospel of Christ like never before.

Creation itself is teaming with revelation about the life of Jesus. The Earth, universe, plants and creatures tell their own story of sin and redemption. It's amazing that these are included in God's plan for salvation as He came to save the world because He loved every aspect of what He'd created. In the book of Romans there's an alluring verse that allows us to see creation's part in the gospel of Christ:

> *For the creation waits in eager expectation for the children of God to be revealed.*[124]

Here, creation is shown to be alive with anticipation and longing for God's redemption to become complete. The gospel of Christ is wide enough to redeem the whole universe and unique enough to affect one person at a time. As we live, observe and experience life on all sorts of levels, we're able to walk into the revelation of Jesus.

---

[124] Romans 8:19 NIV

Life's Experiences

Our perspective on life will depend on our personality and culture, among other things. It's the *glass half empty* or *half full* approaches. When it comes to observing life in the light of the gospel, I'd like to suggest that contemplating both the negative and positive elements of our experience have their lessons. The Bible itself is a mixture of lamentations and celebrations—to ignore one or the other can limit our understanding of what Jesus has accomplished.

Observing Sin

We certainly don't want to dwell on sin and how awful our world can be. Sometimes I feel the need to monitor how much bad news I listen to, as it can have an adverse effect upon my wellbeing.

Unfortunately their are some doom-and-gloom Christians that see sin crouching around every corner. They're often quick to point out the sin in other people's' lives and use Jesus as the excuse in doing so. This is a far cry from who we are meant to be as followers of Christ. We're meant to be light-bearers; people who carry the solutions and give them freely away. People who love others out of the things that imprison them. People who bring a revolution of kindness.

However, it's impossible to live life without seeing sin's corruption in people, institutions and the environment. And we need to learn how to use this level of observation to fuel us into the right direction.

As we watch the corrupt and broken elements of our society unfold, we need to let this knowledge align us with the need for the gospel of Jesus. The more sin we see, the more we should be convicted of the world's need for Jesus.

Witnessing Goodness

While observing sin can re-emphasize the need for Jesus, witnessing goodness in people can align us with Jesus' cause.

I love the term *original goodness*. It's a perspective changer—the other side of the coin. While we know that the world has been corrupted by sin, we also know that we were made in the image of God, and that God is good. While we wrestle with all sorts of selfishness and evil, humankind also has spectacular moments where flickers of God's goodness can be seen. Whether people know God or not, His imprint can still be seen in people as they choose (often against all odds) to overcome and love selflessly. Displays of goodness need to fire up our passion for people and inspire hope in us for Jesus' cause.

Jesus' cause is to call people out of darkness into light. He carries a ridiculous amount of hope for each person. Jesus doesn't focus on the darkness that can shroud a person's life. Instead, He seeks out the light in each of us – no matter how small – and ushers it into growth.

> *For the testimony of Jesus is the spirit of prophecy.*[125]

---

125 Revelation 19:10 KJV

Jesus' cause models the spirit of prophecy, because the spirit of prophecy is one which seeks out the goodness in people and speaks life over a person to free them to be all that they were created to be. We see this happen when Jesus calls Simon to be one of His disciples. In John's gospel we are shown how Jesus renames Simon to Peter:

> *And he brought him to Jesus. Jesus looked at him and said, "You are Simon son of John. You will be called Cephas" (which, when translated, is Peter).*[126]

The significance of this lies in the meanings of the names. The name Simon means 'broken reed' and the name Peter means 'rock'. Jesus calls Simon into his destiny. Translated into layman terms, Jesus is saying to Peter 'the world calls you a broken reed, but I see who you really are, and I call you the rock.' Jesus is modeling the spirit of prophecy which sees *who a person is created to be* and calls that person out.

We have a choice as to what grabs our attention, and where our natural focus is inclined. As we observe life unfold all around us and interact with all sorts of people throughout our days, we can choose to be overwhelmed with how bad things are, or we can join Jesus' cause and see the original good in people and creation. The more we see the original good the more we will carry a passion for redemption, which is the passion of Christ. Instead of feeling despair for people and our world, we will join Jesus in carrying an absurd amount of hope.

---

126   John 1:41 NIV

Death

Where, O death, is your victory? Where, O death, is your sting? [127]

I was 11 when I had my first experience of death. My best friend Hannah tragically died in an accident in Turkey. She was on vacation with her family and as she stood on the balcony of her apartment, it collapsed beneath her.

We'd been born in the same hospital and our mothers had met and become friends around our birth. For my first 11 years my life was happily intertwined with Hannah's.

Up until that point, death wasn't a real concept to me. I knew that people died but it was as if death was just some far off myth that happened to others. When we found out about Hannah's death we were on vacation ourselves in the quaint seaside village of Llangrannog in West Wales. Strangely, that morning, I remember watching the news on TV as they reported an accident of some teenage girls in Turkey. They didn't mention the names and the thought whizzed through my mind that I hoped Hannah was okay as I knew she was there. But that was it, I soon forgot about the news that morning. I spent the day playing on the sand, swimming in the sea and eating ice-cream without a care in the world.

Later that evening I was taking a bath and my mother knocked the door asking if I was almost done. It was then,

---

127   1 Corinthians 15: 54-55 NIV

that moment before anything else was said that I knew that Hannah had died. I sat in that bath and told my mum I'd be out soon, but I knew that as I left that bathroom, she would take me and tell me that my best friend had died.

Hannah knew Jesus in a real way. We'd both attended church groups together for years and a passion for Jesus was firmly rooted in her heart. We'd both prayed prayers that asked Jesus to come into our lives. For me as an 11-year-old, Hannah's death had a profound effect on how I understood the life of Jesus. For the first time in my life as I was faced with the death of my friend, I found myself knowing the true extent of how Jesus had conquered death, and strangely, hope trumped fear in that moment for me.

The night I found out about Hannah's death I had an open vision:

I woke up in the middle of the night and saw Hannah in the corner of my room. She was glorious, shining and beautiful. She looked at me and said *"Ruth, listen to me. Don't worry about me—I'm in an incredible place. But for you, you need to remember to fight the good fight of the faith, take hold of the eternal life that Jesus has given you and continue to tell people about Jesus."* And then she was gone. She was quoting 1 Timothy 6:12. It was a favorite verse of hers—one that was written on a bookmark in her Bible.

I certainly don't believe that God caused Hannah's death—I believe that she was meant to live out her full life like any other person. I believe that Satan snatched her life before her time. However, I also experienced first-hand how God could weave in and out of this horrific event to bring His glory. For me, eternal life became real as an 11 year old. I was so thankful to Jesus for His sacrifice because it meant that one day I'd get to hang out with my friend again, and this time there would be no separation. A sharp realization of the fleeting nature of life and the urgency for people to experience the good news of Jesus gripped my heart.

No one wants to be confronted with death. There's a God-given desire in us to fight for life. However, as we live out our days, we will face death and we need to know that there's treasure to be found even in those dark and painful times.

The best insight God has given me about this dynamic is from the Bible's story of Samson. Samson shares a riddle with his thirty wedding companions: *"Out of the eater, something to eat; out of the strong, something sweet."* and challenges them to solve it. It's not the riddle itself that imparts wisdom—more the story that precedes it. It's a short account of Samson finding the carcass of a lion that he had earlier killed—a young lion that had tried to kill him as he approached the vineyards of Timnah. When he returned and found the carcass he saw that a swarm of bees had made honey inside it, which he in turn scooped out and ate. It's this story that sets the foundations for his famous riddle. The reason this speaks to me so much it's striking picture of how God can work through the darkest of times. He's the God of the turn-around—the One who can create something sweet out of something that stinks of death.

The honey that I've found is a honey that reaffirms the victorious truth of the gospel of Jesus. It's sweet even in the hardest times. Since Hannah, I've encountered the death of a loved one or friend on a number of occasions, and each time as I ride the gut wrenching waves of sadness and grief, I also experience my faith in Jesus being firmly established. Through these seasons I've wrestled with my faith, and as a consequence, become more certain of my eternal future.

> *Now faith is confidence in what we hope for and assurance about what we do not see.*[128]

The gospel of Jesus Christ is being continually revealed to us. If we embrace the nature of this revelation and understand that it's meaning is to be found in life all around us, we will grow in our understanding and ultimately our passion for His gift.

A Gift you Want to Share

Through our years of marriage I've honed the art of buying the right gifts for my husband Chris. In the early days it was a disaster, as I would regularly buy him things that I thought he would like, but it was always difficult for me to tell if I'd scored with a gift or not, since Chris isn't typically charismatic in his expressions. His immediate response with a gift seemed to be the same whether he really liked it or not. My responses are entirely different.

I find it almost impossible not to show my true feelings through my physical demeanor. My responses are extreme;

---

[128] Hebrews 1:11 NIV

overjoyed if it's something I really want, and silent if actually I'm planning to take it back. But with Chris I could never really know in the moment he opened a gift whether I'd got it right. What I've come to learn though is that I can tell if it's a win with what happens to the gift in the following few weeks.

One year in the early days of our marriage I bought him a calligraphy set. (It was a good one too!) I honestly thought this was a clever, well-thought-out gift. Chris had repeatedly told me this story of how, when he was in high school, the only person that encouraged him was his art teacher who pointed out that he was really good at calligraphy. From that spurned a career in art and design and he seemed to relate a lot of meaning to that time of his life.

So when I presented this gift to him one Christmas morning I was a little perplexed when I got the *"thanks babe"* as he placed it on the floor and didn't even look inside the box. Not only that, but a few years later when we were selling our house and we were packing up and clearing out, there I found the calligraphy set—in the same unopened state as it was that Christmas morning.

You see, for Chris, if he's passionate about a gift he doesn't jump up and down with excitement, what he does do is *use it all the time.* And that's how I know. If it's left on the shelf collecting dust like that overpriced calligraphy set, then I haven't got it right. But if he quietly but consistently uses it, it's something that he's greatly appreciated.

As we think of gaining a passion for the gospel of Jesus, it's critical we note that this can be expressed in many different ways—often according to the person's personality. We can make the mistake of thinking that passion always has to be visible and charismatic, but that's a judgment that simply isn't accurate. Passion for someone or something is expressed in what we talk about, how we spend our time and how we use our resources. Passion produces an energy and fervor about those things, but it isn't always charismatic in behavior. While passion can exude outward expressions, those expressions aren't always the marker of what's going on in the heart. So caution is needed with our assumptions.

The real evidence of passion for Jesus' gospel is the fruit of someone's life. *How are they loving their neighbors? What are they doing with their time? How are they living out this good news?* These things are the overflow of a heart seized by a holy affection for what Jesus has done.

A sure sign of a passion for the gospel of Jesus is how much someone shares it with others. It becomes such 'good news' in your life that you simply want everyone to experience it too.

One of the best weddings I've ever attended was one of my friends', Zoe and George. They got married on the picturesque cliffs of The Gower in Wales. It was stunning; a beautiful old stone church with stained glass windows that flooded the church with streams of sunlight. Zoe, who already is a beauty, was of course even more beautiful that day. But the one thing that stood out and was the topic of discussion the following day was the speech that George's grandfather made as he imparted his wisdom to the newlyweds.

He used this important 15 minutes of their wedding service

to communicate that the most important thing of all in life is that all hope is found in Jesus. He commended this to the couple for their marriage and he offered this advice to the congregation too. I've heard plenty of evangelists preach but this was nothing like any of those. There were no slick funny stories, no quick routes to Jesus. Instead it was as if Jesus simply poured out of him.

The Bible says that it's out of the heart that the mouth speaks [129]. George's grandfather's heart was seized by a Holy passion for Jesus. It was authentic and pure. Sharing the good news of Jesus comes easy to those who are passionate about Him.

People evangelize all the time about things that have changed their life; whether health and fitness, the places they live, the schools that their kids attend, sports or spirituality. It's natural to share the things that really matter to you. People who carry a passion for the gospel of Jesus naturally share his goodness authentically to those around them.

A passion for Jesus' gospel starts when you experience His grace and salvation on a personal level for the first time. From there, it's an ever-evolving road full of life's twists and turns where this 'good news' sinks in deeper and deeper. Ultimately, people who are passionate about the gospel of Jesus want others to know it's available for them also.

---

129   Luke 6:45

A Passion for Prophecy

Follow the way of love and eagerly desire gifts of the Spirit, especially prophecy.[130]

The Bible encourages us to have a passion for the prophetic. The Apostle Paul teaches the church in Corinth to 'eagerly desire' prophecy. This should at least get our attention. This suggests to us that the gift of prophecy is good—*really* good. Paul doesn't stop there—he unpacks this even further:

For he who speaks in a tongue does not speak to men but to God, for no one understands him; however, in the spirit he speaks mysteries. But he who prophesies speaks edification and exhortation and comfort to men. He who speaks in a tongue edifies himself, but he who prophesies edifies the church.[131]

This gift of the Holy Spirit – prophecy – that brings forth the now Word of God is an amazing asset to the church. Paul explains this by showing how prophecy brings edification, exhortation and comfort to the people of God.

It's important to unpack this language that Paul uses and let it impact ourselves. Sometimes we can get overly familiar with these classic scriptures and not get the full whack of their meaning.

---

130 1 Corinthians 14:1 NIV
131 1 Corinthians 14:2-4 NKJV

Let's look at some of the definitions of these words and their associated meanings. Paul uses three words to describe the effects of the prophetic gift; edification, exhortation and comfort.

1. Edification

The definition of this word is to 'instruct, uplift or benefit especially morally or spiritually'. Some of its synonyms are; enlighten, improve, educate and teach. This is the first word that Paul uses to describe to the Corinthian church the reason why prophecy is so good.

2. Exhortation

The definition of this word is 'an utterance, discourse, or address conveying urgent advice or recommendations.' The nature of this urgent advice is found in some of the Word's synonyms; encouragement, advice, counsel and caution.

3. Comfort

Finally, Paul uses the word *comfort*. Other words that are associated with this are; happiness, relief, restfulness, well-being and cheerfulness. These are great commendations for the prophetic gift and great things for any church to have. The beginnings of developing a passion for the prophetic starts right here, with this knowledge that this gift is very very good.

Understanding, Learning and Practice - A Good Foundation

Developing a passion for the prophetic is way more than being obsessed with it. Instead it's cultivating a deep admiration for how God uses the prophetic and the fruit that the prophetic word brings.

If you're interested in becoming passionate about the prophetic, you can start by learning about it. There are plenty of books on the topic that clearly unpack what prophecy is and what it's for. The first book I read on prophecy was Mike Bickle's *Growing in the Prophetic* over 15 years ago. This was my first significant entry point into understanding the prophetic gift and how it could be something for me. From there I've read lots of books on prophecy and attended lots of courses on the topic.

As you gain knowledge of the prophetic it's important that you get involved with it personally. Learning about it without experiencing it will only get you so far.

When I developed my own courses on prophecy, I built-in a stipulation that *whoever attended would also agree to be on my prophetic teams for 6 months*. This ensured that the person would gain intellectual understanding, but also practice the gift so they knew it personally. Once you begin to receive a prophetic word and also give a prophetic word, your relationship with prophecy has much more meaning.

Receiving prophetic words is an empowering part of being a

Christian. At home, I have a file full of prophetic words given to me throughout my life by various Christians Every few months I pull it out and reread what's been said. Some of it has come forth and some is yet to come. I hold onto it lightly, and yet I do hold onto it.

When I was 29 I decided to travel to the U.S. on my own to see what God was doing in other churches. I went for a month, and during that time as I visited churches, I received a lot of prophecy. Sometimes I was called out in a meeting, other times I went and asked someone ministering to prophesy over me. At the end of this trip I met Chris, who is now my husband. I know this was a pivotal time for me and those words of affirmation and encouragement were crucial in setting me on the right path.

When I was pregnant with Titus my friends threw a baby shower. Among all the lovely gifts people brought to celebrate the birth of my first son, the most treasured to me were the prophetic words each of my friends brought for Titus. This was something I specifically requested, and I remember a few of them feeling a little overwhelmed—especially those who hadn't been used to the prophetic gift. I encouraged them to keep it simple and just ask God to give them something.

Amazingly enough they all had something to bring. What was incredible to me was that all the words fitted perfectly together like a jigsaw puzzle. It was a lovely experience as they shared what God had put on their hearts.

Receiving prophetic words will give you a passion for prophecy. As you get words of affirmation, confirmation and future hope you'll witness first-hand how loving a Father we have and how wonderful this gift is.

But it's also important that you take the risk and start asking God to speak to you with prophetic words for others. I firmly believe that the gift of prophecy is meant for all believers. I believe God speaks to all people, and if we take the time to ask Him, He will use us to bring encouragement to others.

The Thrill of Seeing Lives Changed

The thing that will catapult you from *admiring the prophetic gift* from a distance to *being fully passionate for it* will be this: seeing lives transformed.

When I left my position as the prophetic pastor to move to the U.S., I remember sitting down and reflecting. I'd been in ministry for over 10 years within our church and I was able to look back over the work I'd done with a critical eye and a clean spirit. There were certain things that I was convinced that I would do over and over again. One of these things was to encourage, teach and practice prophecy.

I remember specifically saying to myself during this season *"I love the prophetic gift."* The reason for this wasn't because I was well-read on the prophetic, nor was it because it was my niche for many years. It was simply because I'd witnessed countless people who'd had their lives improved, encouraged and transformed by this precious gift. It was addictive to see how the sweet the fruit of this gift could be.

One of the most encouraging emails I've received was from a lady in our church who wrote to me 2 years after I'd shared a prophetic word during a Sunday service. I'd had a picture of the scales of justice in which the scales had been weighed down on the wrong side. In this picture I saw God's hands drop coins into the other side of the scales with a promise to bring justice.

I vaguely remember sharing this. What I didn't know at the time was how significant this picture was to this lady. Her email informed me that her marriage had been falling apart, and her desire to have children seemed lost as she looked at her future. This picture, however, blasted her with hope that transcended human logic. It gave her a sense that God the Father was at work, and no matter how bleak things appeared, He was about to tip the scales in her favor. She continued to disclose the fact God had indeed been faithful—her marriage had survived and they were that weekend dedicating their first child to God!

Stories like this make my heart rejoice, and make me want to pursue the prophetic gift even more. What I've come to realize is that people everywhere need to hear the Father's voice.

One of the most unusual places I've ministered in the prophetic is at Glastonbury Festival in the UK. "Glastonbury" is a famous music festival that's held every year in Somerset. A couple hundred thousand party-goers turn up and camp for 4 days of music, drinking and partying.

I began attending this festival through a ministry that my colleagues and dear friends Greg & Clare Thompson had set up. It was a Christian art venue for the festival called *elemental*. At the time it was the only official 'Christian' venue of the festival, and was possibly the best ministry I've ever been a part of. Each year there was a team of around 40 Christians who would each bring their own unique gifts to the venue. The venue itself was a giant marquis, artistically decorated by a genius team of Christian artists. It was a retreat in the middle of the Glastonbury buzz that boasted comfy sofas and hot cups of tea - a place that homed the kindness of Christ.

I remember the first year I was part of this team. It was also the first year I'd ever been to the festival. It was so eye-opening. The creativity there is breathtaking with costumes, villages, stilt-walkers and fire-breathers. As well as being one of the most famous music festivals in the world, Glastonbury was also deeply spiritual.

I remember walking through the 'healing fields' where the smell of incense was strong as I wandered through the marketplace of new age spirituality. I understood that this was a place where everything was up for grabs—there was an openness here that people would embrace for the 4 days of 'free living' before they went back to their office jobs on Monday morning.

After a few years of being part of the team, we talked about offering prophecy to the festival-goers. Our venue *elemental* had been known for it's quirky ventures in the past; free hair washing, dream interpretation, comedy skits, healing as well as its first-rate music program and feisty late-night discussions. There were already a number of people on the team who were well-versed in the prophetic, so we cobbled together a sign saying *Free Future Telling* and trained a handful of the team to listen to God for any people who wanted it.

The first year we started 'future telling' at Glastonbury I was blown away by the hunger of 'un-churched' people to hear from God, and the grace that the Holy Spirit poured upon us through the gift of prophecy. We were no prophecy superstars, that was for sure – we were simply willing to take the risk to hear from God for strangers – and yet I have never seen the prophetic gift so strong and accurate. Some of the team had never prophesied before, and yet here they were pouring out words of gold to the unsuspecting punters.

I distinctly recall a group of six girls that entered the venue. I watched as they dared each other to get some "future telling"—more as a joke than anything else. They picked up their 'free future-telling tokens' and shyly approached, while looking back to their friends smirking in the corner. We explained our approach:

> *We are Christians. We believe that God loves you and is really interested in your future and He loves to encourage us. So we will listen to Him for you and share what we get. Nothing will be doom and gloom, just things to encourage you.*

Within five minutes of sharing words, both girls were in tears. Good tears. Shocked tears. We'd touched on a deep issue that only they and their friends knew, upon which God spoke healing and hope. They ran back to their friends urging them to get some too. *"It's real"* I heard one of them say. Over the course of 4 days we prophesied over hundreds of festival-goers. Many tears were shed and much hope was given.

It's stories like this that make me passionate for the prophetic Word. This gift releases people to become who they're meant to be. It puts a fire in people's spirit and fills them with the Father's love... and it's stunning to watch. This is why I always make room in my life to prophesy. Whether I've been a prophetic pastor or a full-time mom—I've disciplined myself to carve out time to hear from the Father through the Spirit's gift so that I can see one more person transformed by His words.

If you're looking to be a person who becomes passionate about prophecy, throw yourself into it's teaching, receive prophetic words and most importantly, take the risk to hear from God for others. Once you begin to see the power of this gift up-close and personal, you'll begin to love, cherish and honor it.

I believe there's going to be a reawakened passion for the Word. Men and women whose hearts are overwhelmed by scripture, people who have a passion for Jesus and a new maturity to the *now* Word that comes through the Holy Spirit—the gift of prophecy.

When I look to the future and see the challenges that will be set against my children's' spiritual journeys, I long to leave them a legacy of wisdom—foundational, unshakable truths that will help them navigate in an increasingly complex society. Their journey is one that only they can walk, but I want to give them an inheritance of being steadfast in their footing. With the Word as one foot and the Spirit as the other, my hope is that they will find authentic faith and a freedom to express it.

7
passion for the spirit

The church for too long has followed Casper, the friendly ghost instead of seeking the fire of the Holy Spirit. We have turned limp at the thought of our own cross; we faint when we think of suffering or sacrifice. Beloved, it is time to embrace the fire of God's Presence. It is the fire that purifies our sacrifice. [132]

Getting Past Fear

We will never be passionate about the things we fear. We might be obsessed, but never passionate because passion evolves from a deep love, and there's no love in Fear. Fear usually creates a distance from the thing, person or idea that it fears, and it becomes impossible to even begin a passionate journey with it.

This is why the starting point for developing a passion for the

---

[132] Francis Frangipane, frangipane.org/ffquotes

Holy Spirit is to get real with the fears that some people have of Him. Unless we do this, these people don't have a chance of walking into the freedom and the fruit that the Holy Spirit brings.

This isn't the type of fear that's actually awe. There's a Biblical precedent of that type of fear that's present because of the Holiness of God. The Bible sometimes calls it 'the fear of the Lord'. One of the great evangelists of the 20th century, Mordecai Ham, describes this sense of overwhelming awe in God's presence:

> *I had an overwhelming experience of the Lord's presence. I felt so powerfully overcome by the nearness of the Holy Spirit that I had to ask the Lord to draw back lest He kill me. It was so glorious that I couldn't stand more than a small portion of it.*[133]

Even though this type of experience can be scary, it's so grounded in truth and love that it causes the person to draw closer to God rather than remain distant. The fear that we're addressing is a human fear where suspicion and mistrust rule the day, forcing a great chasm between the person and the Holy Spirit. It's the ultimate deception of Satan to cause a Christian to fear the Holy Spirit in this way—causing a separation from the very person of God who means to bring us freedom and fruitfulness.

It takes great humility to overcome this type of fear because

---

133   Mordecai Ham, Establishing the Kingdom of God, Daryl Allen, p126

most people who fear the Spirit are steeped in belief that they are right to do so. It's not as if they haven't thought about it—layers of reasons as to why they should steer clear have accumulated over years of experiences. It also doesn't help that many "spirit-filled" believers can exhibit very little patience for people who are suspect of them.

It's vital that we understand where this type of fear comes from. Where does it get its foothold? What are the keys to overcoming it?

Up Close and Personal vs Distance Learning

I remember having a conversation one day with one of my best friends. She disclosed to me that when she first met me she, was scared and intimidated by me! I remember being really shocked. *What? Why?*

At the time I was a feisty young leader at church and would regularly preach at Sunday services. The first year I met her we didn't have much of a personal connection. The only interaction I had with her was in a group or at church. She witnessed me from a distance and saw a representation of my personality in the most unusual way – me preaching – and this intimidated her.

It was a great conversation to have with a true friend. We were able to talk about how easy it is to be misrepresented by public roles. We talked about the insecurities that existed in my friend that made her want to run away from me. We talked about the need and responsibility I had to communicate who I am to people in ways that were more understandable.

One of the greatest revelations that came through this conversation, though, was that personal relationship was needed to undo this misunderstanding. As we spent time together in those early days and became deep friends, she realized that I was not someone she needed to fear. In fact, she realized I would become her biggest fan. I would lay my life down for her and do anything to cheer her on and help her succeed.

This truth applies to how we approach the Holy Spirit. If we've only ever gotten to know Him from a distance without having embraced a personal relationship with Him, we will be open to all sorts of misinterpretation of who He is and what He does. We can easily be intimated, suspicious and scared of Him because *seeing Him from a distance* is a flawed way of understanding who He is. We're simply not meant to get to know the Spirit like this. It has to start from a personal relationship with Him. When we embrace Him as a friend, all our misgivings will disintegrate as we begin to see Him for who He is.

Getting to know the Holy Spirit from a distance, without any personal interaction with Him, is dangerous ground. It's unsafe territory where Satan – who is like a thief – is waiting to capitalize on every weakness we may have as the Spirit is presented to us.

Fear of the Spirit can be present because of our own insecurities. Usually the last place we look to unpack why we would carry this type of fear is ourselves. Instead we prefer to build a case for why we believe what we believe. Soul searching can be a painful process. It's hard to admit that we have weaknesses, unwhole patterns of behavior and insecurities that can be reasons for ignoring or distorting truth.

Have you ever had a friend point out your faults? How do you react? I'm notoriously bad at responding to this kind of challenge. I've had it happen to me a number of times and each time my immediate response has been quite disappointing—I feel hurt and get incredibly defensive.

I remember one instance when I was attending a staff retreat for my church. It was a time carved out of the annual diary for input and encouragement. There was a session where we wanted to share what we believed God was saying to each other—encouragements for our ministries. One by one, people were getting affirmed by these words of endorsement. Then someone came to me and began to share:

"I see you being like the fingernail on the finger of God..."

'Awesome' I thought. Clearly I was significant to God, His powerful little weapon.

"...You've been positioned right in the center of what God's doing now..."

Yes. That's so true. I'm on the cutting edge—a radical, I mused to myself.

"...You just need to be careful you don't scratch people..."

Wait. What? What did you just say? You think I scratch people? I don't scratch people!

I could feel my neck going bright red and I broke out with stress. A lump formed in my throat. Noise buzzed in my brain like someone was trying to change a station in my head and I couldn't gather any sensible thoughts. I was silent, I knew if I opened my mouth I would be a blubbering mess. I sat there wishing the time would go quickly so I could run away and hide.

For the following few days I criticized the approach of this person. We teach that prophecy is meant be encouraging and uplifting—how then was this right? They were clearly in the wrong. They should never have brought something negative into a time that was meant to be affirming.

As I continued to build a case for this in my mind I happened to read this verse in the bible

> *Open rebuke is better*
> *Than love carefully concealed.*
> *Faithful are the wounds of a friend,*
> *But the kisses of an enemy are deceitful* [134]

This verse made me pause. It seemed there was some cause for rebuke where there was deep friendship. Rebuke out of love.

---

[134] Psalm 27:5-6 NASB

My feathers were still ruffled though.

I had a long conversation with my friend and colleague Clare about this. I think we were on the phone for almost two hours that day. She listened patiently as I poured out my feelings. Clare was fantastic in this conversation and she gave me counsel that really shaped my life. She was gently suggested that I had two options. Option one was to believe that the person made a mistake, forgive them and move on. Option two was to bravely ask God whether there was any bit of truth in what was said. She remained impartial but I could sense that she knew that option two, although the harder option, was the one that would bring victory all round. And so it was during this season of my life that I began to know the true benefit of praying the prayer that the psalmist prays to God.

> *Search me, O God, and know my heart;*
> *Try me, and know my anxieties;*
> *And see if there is any wicked way in me,*
> *And lead me in the way everlasting.*[135]

And of course as God searched me, there were things in my life that I needed to look at. *Overlooking people for the sake of vision* was one that I'd just not been aware of. A blind spot in my life. But God used this hard moment, He grounded it in the safety of friendship and worked to make me a much better me.

When I think back upon this instance and others like it,

---

[135] Psalm 139:23-24 NKJV

I realize that – even though these have been some of my most painful times – they've also been the most significant moments of my journey with God. And I've come to know this truth; allowing God to search you for any broken, sinful patterns of behavior and thought is the most direct route to freedom. It's often raw, it's humbling but it gets you to freedom's side quickly.

If you're a person whose skeptical of the Holy Spirit because of what you've seen from a distance, it's important to contemplate whether or not there's something within yourself that's allowing this fear to fester. It's a simple but difficult prayer; *God, search me.* But it remains a foolproof prayer that searches out truth. And most people I've met who keep their distance from the Spirit are actually people who love truth.

> *Ultimately we know deeply that the other side of every fear is freedom.*[136]

Building a Foundation of Truth

Getting past the fear of the Spirit begins with the revelation that Satan will use anything to misrepresent the Spirit. He will keep us at a distance, use the flaws of others and exploit our own weaknesses.

Gaining that revelation puts us onto the right path because we start questioning the validity of this fear. This alone will loosen

136 Marilyn Ferguson

its grip. The next thing to do is fully embrace what Jesus taught about the Spirit's role; this will build a foundation of truth. We need set aside our bad experiences of other people's expression of Him and simply go back to the source of scripture to examine the truth of who the Spirit is.

One of Jesus' teachings to the multitudes was how an unclean spirit can return with seven other evil spirits if nothing replaces the space it once occupied:

> *When an unclean spirit goes out of a man, he goes through dry places, seeking rest; and finding none, he says, 'I will return to my house from which I came.' And when he comes, he finds it swept and put in order. Then he goes and takes with him seven other spirits more wicked than himself, and they enter and dwell there; and the last state of that man is worse than the first.*[137]

This wisdom is something that's vital to grasp when breaking free from a fear of the Holy Spirit. By realizing that this fear is not from God, we are essentially tearing down an old mindset. In order for that mindset to not return, it's imperative that we replace it with a foundation of truth. In this case, it's going back scripture to fully grapple with the truth of who the Holy Spirit is and what it means for us to have Him live in us.

Scripture is specific about the role of the Spirit—it doesn't present a cautious middle ground. It's not shy to hold the Holy Spirit up as the great glorious gift, or as a precious gift

---

137   Luke 11:24-26 NKJV

to us from the Father. When you read scripture it becomes an absurd notion that anyone who believes in Jesus would be cautious of the Spirit. Why? Because the Holy Spirit is God Himself.

The classic passages in scripture where Jesus talks about the Holy Spirit to His disciples are found in the gospel of John. This is right before Jesus' ascension;

> *But now I go away to Him who sent Me, and none of you asks Me, 'Where are You going?' But because I have said these things to you, sorrow has filled your heart. Nevertheless I tell you the truth. It is to your advantage that I go away; for if I do not go away, the Helper will not come to you; but if I depart, I will send Him to you. And when He has come, He will convict the world of sin, and of righteousness, and of judgment: of sin, because they do not believe in Me; of righteousness, because I go to My Father and you see Me no more; of judgment, because the ruler of this world is judged.*
>
> *I still have many things to say to you, but you cannot bear them now. However, when He, the Spirit of truth, has come, He will guide you into all truth; for He will not speak on His own authority, but whatever He hears He will speak; and He will tell you things to come. He will glorify Me, for He will take of what is Mine and declare it to you. All things that the Father has are Mine. Therefore I said that He will take of Mine and declare it to you.*[138]

---

[138] John 16:5-15 NKJV

Jesus describes the Holy Spirit to His disciples in many ways; the Helper, the Spirit of Peace, and the Spirit of Truth. But perhaps the best commendation that Jesus gives the Holy Spirit is Jesus' insistence that it was better for the disciples that Jesus leaves so that the Holy Spirit would come.

Jesus was called Immanuel, meaning *God with us*. This truth was the greatest thing that had ever happened to mankind. But now it was to progress from Jesus – God *with* us – to The Holy Spirit who would be God *in* us. There was to be no distance and no separation from God for God's children.

Getting to Know the Spirit

I met my husband in Pomona, California. I'd been traveling across the United States visiting churches and my penultimate stop was LA. I'd never met Chris before, but I ended up staying at his house because I knew his house-mate who'd kindly offered to put me up. The first night I met Chris I saw him for 5 minutes. I'd only just arrived at the house and it was nearing midnight. We simply said hi and I thanked him for letting me stay.

That night I dreamt that Chris had moved to England, he'd become a huge part of my life and knew all my friends and family. I woke up feeling really perplexed, almost annoyed at the thought of something so ridiculous. However, over the course of that time, it was as if there was a magnetic force pulling us together. By the end of that time he sat me down to tell me his intentions *"I'm going to move to England and marry you!"*

I was 29 years old. As I headed back to England I dreaded all the 'warning' chats my friends and colleagues would give me. I knew how ridiculous this all sounded—*I met a guy and in 10 days we 'just knew'*. But I also knew that I did indeed know this was the man I was to marry.

Chris, true to his word, moved to England 3 months later. He'd given up his job, sold most of his stuff and arrived in Heathrow with a suitcase in tow. During those few months of being apart we'd intensely embraced getting to know as much of each other's lives as possible. These were pre-Facetime days, so we'd signed up on the cheapest international phone contract and we spoke every day. I remember those days with fondness—there was such an appetite in each of us to know every detail about the other. It had become the most important thing.

There was an intensity in those first few months to discover each other. I wanted to know all about this man who was about to be part of my life forever.

At the time of writing, we've been married for almost 9 years and the *getting to know you* part has never really ended. It certainly slows down at times, but as it does so, there's that deep satisfaction of knowing a person in such depth. Plus, there's always moments of surprise. Just when I think I have Chris sussed, he surprises me. The truth is *getting to know a person* never really ends.

The Holy Spirit is a person. He's not some 'mist' or 'thing' that we handle mysteriously. He's the person of God that is here to live in us, and to gain a passion for Him we need to get to know Him.

Just like any other significant relationship, there will be seasons of great intensity and our appetite to know Him will be huge. And then there will be times where we might feel we know His ways and can discern His voice and we will enjoy the privilege of kicking back and knowing God. But because we can never really fully know Him in this lifetime because He is God Himself, we embrace a constant fascinating journey of getting to know the Holy Spirit throughout the course of our lives.

In my own life, I feel very comfortable with the Holy Spirit. I know His voice and I've learned to sense His presence with me. I've also had various seasons of my life where one or more of His gifts have been given to me. There are some gifts that have been a constant companion and others that seem to come and go. And yet even in my comfort with Him, I never take Him for granted. How foolish would that be. Because no matter how long you've been walking with Him, there are always surprises along the way—things that happen that cause a holy fascination to rise within you.

I remember one such moment fondly where the Spirit worked in a way that shook me out of any complacency I had with His ways. I was speaking at a Christian conference in England—a session on prayer. I remember that, halfway through my talk, I felt that I should stop and pray. As I did, I happened to start speaking in tongues (which is one of the gifts of the Holy Spirit).

As an aside—I had spoken in tongues for many years after

hearing some teaching on it—but for me this gift had always been something of a spiritual discipline that the Holy Spirit helped me with. The gift of tongues is simply a spiritual language that you can learn with practice, but also at times have 'downloaded' to you from the Spirit. I know people who've received the gift of tongues as a download, and it's amazing to witness. But up to this point in my life I wasn't one of those people who'd clearly received a download of some heavenly language. But I was okay with that—it didn't make me feel any less worthy. As I spoke in tongues during this talk it was much the same as any other time I'd spoken in tongues. It was just for a few minutes and then I continued with my talk.

Later that day I was approached by a lady who was beaming with joy. She took me aside and filled me in with her story. She'd been in my session on prayer and told me that she'd just come back from Belize while serving as a missionary there for many years. She said that she went to my talk with a heavy heart and was still questioning whether it was right for her to return to England and start a new season of life. She told me that, when I was speaking in tongues, I was actually speaking in Creole, a popular language in Belize and that I had said *"Everything is going to be okay, everything is going to be okay, everything is going to be okay."* She knew that God was using this moment to speak directly to her, and she felt joy flood through her. I was stunned. I thought I'd heard it all, but this was fascinating to me, especially since, on my end, it didn't feel spiritually charged. *Wow, just wow Holy Spirit, your ways are indeed marvelous.*

It's this 'getting to know' journey we have with the Spirit

that's key in producing a passion for Him within ourselves. There's only a handful of people you get to know to this level during the course of a lifetime. Usually a spouse, siblings, children or some lifelong friends. There are, of course, plenty of people we get to know in seasons of life or on a more superficial level. But there's nothing like the people we live with—the people who share our days, see our dirty laundry and witness us in all our colors. These people are the ones who truly know us and whom we truly know. The Holy Spirit doesn't just live in our house, but He lives in our very being. His commitment to us is never ending and He will be the most important person we will ever get to know.

The people you get to know on this level are the people for whom you become willing to lay down your life. There's a charged passion that comes from this committed course of knowing someone that causes a loyalty beyond other relationships.

If we understand that the Holy Spirit is our number one person – the one who will live in us and be committed to us forever – then we will embrace a path that will evoke a remarkable passion to stir in our hearts for Him.

So my commendation to you, if you're serious about gaining a passion for the Spirit, is to embrace this adventure of getting to know Him as your number one. Realize that He's the closest person you're going to ever have in your life this side of heaven, and begin to learn all about His ways.

There are so many facets of getting to know the Holy Spirit and it would be impossible to cover them all in this chapter.

However, I would like to hold up three foundational areas that have been instrumental for me as I've walked out this journey.

1. Getting to Know His Voice

Getting to know the Spirit begins with getting to know His voice. It's impossible to get to know someone without being able to communicate with them. Two things I learned awhile ago now, and which has changed my whole approach to the Holy Spirit, is that He's always speaking and He speaks to everyone. There was a time when I believed that the Spirit would only speak on very special occasions, and to very special people. How wrong I was! The Spirit, who is our best friend and partner, speaks to us throughout each and every day during the course of our entire lives. The trouble is that many Christians haven't trained their ear to recognize His voice. When we begin to learn these things, the realization can come that the Spirit has been speaking to us our whole life, but we just didn't know it was Him.

Discovering the Spirit's Language

Being married to an American and living in America has thrown me into a new culture, and at times a new language. It's amazing how much language is different here in the States when compared to England. I still get blank stares from people as I say some English word that they've never heard before. Trash can / rubbish bin, trunk of the car / boot of the car, candy / sweets, diapers / nappies. The list goes on and on. It always provides some mild entertainment. What I've noticed though, is how I've embraced being an American-English person and how I quite automatically use

American-English to my American friends and revert to English-English with my British friends. Here in Colorado, I'm a 'mom', but when I return to Bristol I'm most definitely a 'mum'. It would've been strange if I hadn't adapted to my environment and sought not only to be understood by my American friends & family, but also to understand their ways and their language.

When it comes to getting to know the Spirit's voice, the first thing we need to know is that He speaks in multiple ways. It's vital that we're open to learning what those are and seek to understand Him in those areas.

I love unpacking all the different ways the Holy Spirit speaks to us as Christians. So often people think He's not speaking to them because they assume that He only speaks audibly, and if that doesn't happen for them, they count themselves out. This can be a result of sloppy spiritual language and a lack of teaching on the Holy Spirit.

I love watching people as they begin to understand the truth that the Holy Spirit speaks in many ways. When people realize this, it opens the door to a life full of conversation with God Himself.

The Spirit speaks to us using our senses, and while He can use all of our senses to communicate, in my experience the main two senses that the Spirit uses are our sight and our hearing. We see examples of this throughout scripture.

Spiritual Seeing

The ways that the Holy Spirit communicates to us through spiritual sight are usually spiritual dreams, open visions, visions of the imagination, creation, angels and circumstances.

We witness Him communicating this way throughout scripture in countless examples in both the Old and New Testaments of people receiving God's advice or instruction.

In the Old Testament, Abraham has a vision where God reaffirmed His covenant with him, reminding him that he would have a son:

> *After these things the word of the Lord came to Abram in a vision: "Fear not, Abram, I am your shield; your reward shall be very great."* [139]

Jacob has a dream of a ladder reaching heaven, where angels ascended and descended. Joseph, perhaps the one most known for his dreams and interpretation of dreams, has a dream showing him the distant future where his brothers bow down to him. It's a dream from God where Solomon chooses wisdom when asked what he wanted:

> *At Gibeon the Lord appeared to Solomon in a dream by night, and God said, "Ask what I shall give you."* [140]

---

[139] Genesis 15:1 ESV
[140] 1 Kings 3:5 ESV

In the New Testament, crucial dreams are given to Joseph about the birth of Jesus, and of Pilate's wife warning her not to kill Jesus. Visions are plentiful with Zacharias, Ananias, Cornelius, Peter, Paul and John all receiving them.

For today, the Holy Spirit uses people's 'sight' to communicate His heart. I remember making a choice very early-on in my faith to be open to the fact that the Holy Spirit could speak to me in this way. As I embraced this 'language', I found the Spirit would speak to me in a myriad of ways involving my spiritual sight.

In 2006 I was involved in leading a young church group. At the time, we were looking for topics to study and one night I had the most peculiar dream. In the dream my mobile phone rang on my bedside table, I answered it and it was my grandmother in heaven. It was most uncanny but she said to me *"Hi darling, listen to me, I don't want you to worry about me, I'm fine, but you must read 1 Thessalonians chapter 4."* Then she hung up and I instantly awoke. In the middle of the night, I picked up my Bible to look at this passage of scripture.

The first half of the chapter unpacked what it looked like to live a life that was pleasing to God. This included a call to live in sexual purity. I knew instantly that this was what we were to study in the group I was leading. As I read the rest of the chapter, I smiled as the Spirit has a way of confirming that I wasn't going crazy. The heading for the final part of 1 Thessalonians, chapter 4 reads:

> *Brothers and sisters, we do not want you to be uninformed about those who sleep in death, so that you do not grieve like*

the rest of mankind, who have no hope.[141]

I have no idea how that dream actually happened. But I do know that the Spirit's intimate knowledge of me found a way to communicate with me in a dream that certainly got my attention, and in some way, strangely brought more peace and joy to my heart about my grandmother's eternal life…

If the Spirit chooses to communicate to you through your sight, you need to be aware of your dreams, mental images, circumstances and the creation of life all around you. He will highlight things to grab your attention. The big question is *will you be watching?*

Spiritual Hearing

Then Jesus said, "Whoever has ears to hear, let them hear."[142]

The Holy Spirit communicates to people using their spiritual hearing. Sometimes He speaks audibly, but most of the time He is the still small voice that speaks to us in our inner being.

While I believe the Spirit *does* speak audibly to people today, just as He did in scripture, I don't believe this particular way of Him speaking is 'elite' prophecy. Unfortunately some Christians measure their level of 'spirituality' on this type of thing. Believing that you've suddenly 'arrived' if you heard the Holy Spirit's audible voice isn't truth.

---

141 1 Thessalonians 4:13 NIV
142 Mark 4:9 NIV

As I've come to understand the languages of the Spirit, His audible voice is one of many ways He communicates. I believe He intrinsically knows us and will speak to us with a language that works with our personality, background and experience.

I've never heard the Spirit's audible voice talking *to* me, but I have heard Him talking to someone else *about* me...

I was away with my friend Abby at a Christian conference. At the end of one of the talks, I decided to go up front to ask the speaker to pray for me. The conference had finished for the day and the crowd was thinning out. Abby was sat in the front row waiting for me. The speaker was Trevor Baker, a prophetically gifted minister who leads 'revival fires' in Dudley, UK. He began to pray for me and the first few minutes he was simply praying God's blessing over my life. I had my eyes closed, since I was intent on receiving all there was to have. Behind, to the left of me, a voice said to Trevor *"ask her what her name is"* and sure enough a few seconds later Trevor asked me what my name was. I said 'Ruth' and it was as if that triggered a whole prophetic word. Trevor prophesied over me using the book of Ruth in the Bible—a significant prophetic word for that season in my life. As we finished, I thanked him and returned to Abby. On my way out, I asked her who was the other person praying standing behind me? She said that there was no one else—that the only people there were myself and Trevor. I was shocked because I knew that I had heard another voice that directed Trevor. I know wholeheartedly that this was the audible voice of the Spirit.

If you open the conversation up to friends that are Christians, it might surprise you how many have, at some moment in their life, heard His audible voice.

The Spirit also speaks to our inner beings. This is often referred to as the inner-voice of God. Sometimes this is loud, sometimes this is quiet, sometimes it's repetitive.

Hearing the inner-voice of the Holy Spirit is something that is wise to learn. It's often how He prompts us, guides us and puts others on our hearts.

This voice isn't always still and small, sometimes it's actually very loud. One time when Chris and I were visiting California, I took a separate trip up north to Redding. I was meeting some friends there at a leaders' conference at Bethel Church. I'd literally been there one day, and as we were out for lunch, I heard the Spirit's inner-voice very loudly say *"call Chris now"*, and it stopped me in my tracks. I phoned Chris and as he answered the phone I knew something wasn't right. He was completely disoriented. I asked him what was wrong and he told me that he'd literally minutes ago been knocked off his bike by a car, he was lying on the ground when I phoned.

The car hadn't stopped and he was left on the side of the road. As you can imagine I was incredibly worried. I was able to phone a close friend of his who immediately went to help him and keep me on the phone as they took him to the emergency room. I also phoned my pastor back in England and asked them to pray for Chris. As it happened, Chris came away with a broken collarbone and, apart from being a bit groggy, was okay for the most part. I'm so grateful though to the Holy Spirit for alerting me to the situation. This proved to be a

Taking Risks

At some point though, the only way to grow in recognizing His voice is to step out and take some risks. When you do this it's either confirmed to be true, or falls flat. Scary I know—but it's here in the practice of sharing His words where we learn huge lessons about His voice.

I remember the first risk I took when I started my own journey of recognizing His voice. I was young and completely inexperienced with the Holy Spirit. I'd been struck that *maybe, just maybe the Holy Spirit does speak to me* but I felt incredibly insecure as to whether or not this was all just in my head. I was in a large city-wide youth worship celebration and during the meeting one of the leaders asked if anyone felt the Holy Spirit speaking to them. Immediately I heard an internal voice

"Hey Ruth, go and share that there's someone here who's in emotional pain that I want to heal. Horses are extremely important to this person."

What!? Please no God that's ridiculous.

"Go on. Go up on stage and share what I've told you."

An argument ensued for a few minutes between the Spirit and I. This was possibly the scariest thing for me—I just felt utterly stupid, but I knew that if I was ever going to find out whether or not this was really the Holy Spirit, I'd have to obey and take a risk. I went and shared this strange word. Lo and behold, the word spoke directly to one person who, as it happened, owned a horse. It was a word of knowledge that the Holy Spirit gives to show people that He knows them intimately, and which can open a door to faith for other things to happen.

Since that day I've never stopped taking risks. I always wrestle with God over a word that He wants me to share - I ask lots of questions; *"Are you sure God? This is definitely you, not me, right?"* But as the years have gone by, my confidence has grown in knowing when it's Him.

Safe to Get it Wrong

Recognizing the Spirit's voice is a learning process. We're not going to immediately know it's Him speaking all the time. His voice is something we get to know over time, and over trial and error. Sometimes, if we get it wrong, it's just as much a learning curve as if we get it right.

Because of this, it's vital that we create safe spaces where we're free to get it wrong. We need safe 'testing grounds' where we can share without causing a disaster.

One of the reasons I set up our 'Prophecy Clinics' at my church in Bristol was to have a place where people could share what they thought the Holy Spirit was saying. During these times, I made sure the folks that came in to receive prophetic words were well-briefed in knowing that *it was their responsibility to discern*, and that our teams could easily get it wrong. Having a policy of *no negative, warning words* also created a safety net within our boundaries. There were surprisingly few times where people got it wrong over the three years I led this ministry. The more they shared accurate words from the Holy Spirit, the more finely-tuned they became in discerning what the Holy Spirit was saying. When they did get it wrong there was no harm done and they were able to take significant steps forward in recognizing the Holy Spirit's voice.

Tuning into His Voice

Hearing the Spirit's voice requires a skill of fine-tuning our ears to recognize it in the midst of life's chaos. Our lives are so full of noise it's easy to simply not see or not hear what the Spirit is saying. I believe He communicates with us all the time, but it's easy to pick up just a tiny portion because we're not sufficiently 'tuned' in.

Being a good listener has never come naturally to me. There have been days when Chris has come home from work and started talking to me, but I've not heard a word he's said. This is an awful trait! But I wonder how much we can do this to the Holy Spirit?

We need to make a choice daily to ask Him what He thinks or what He's saying. We need to acknowledge His presence with us throughout our day. It's this *everyday with the Spirit* that changes us and evokes a passion for Him in our lives.

2. Getting to Know His Personality

> *The Holy Spirit has his own personality. He therefore moves in at will when we least expect it, and sometimes when we*

are least deserving of it.[143]

Many people learn about the Spirit by reading books or going to some teaching seminars, but not all get to know Him—which involves understanding that He is a person and has a personality. It's easy to talk about the Spirit as a commodity; an 'it', 'thing', or 'mist'.

As you get to know the Spirit over time, you'll learn of His personality; you'll pick up what makes Him sad and what makes Him happy. You'll catch the things that are on His heart and discover His sense of humor.

When I was working at Woodlands Church in Bristol, my senior pastor David Mitchell would sometimes be so close to the Spirit that he would pick up the emotions of the Spirit. David is an amazing pastor with an ability to make everyone feel loved and uniquely part of the church. He's pretty funny and often would goof around during staff meetings on his mandolin. His personality is pretty upbeat and usually has everyone laughing when he preaches. But I remember one Sunday morning when he was speaking on how we need to care for the poor in our local community. He could barely speak through the tears. He was manifesting the Holy Spirit's grief. While speaking with him afterwards, he told me that this happens to him on-occasion—where he is overcome by the Spirit's own emotions on a matter.

It's these types of moments – when we're caught up in either

143   R.T. Kendall

the sorrow of the Spirit or the joy of the Spirit – that we glimpse who He is.

As you walk with the Spirit it's important that you take note of your own emotions. Sometimes you will be picking up on what the Holy Spirit is feeling or thinking about. And indeed it's through the time of your relationship with Him that you will get to know His unique personality.

A clue into the Spirit's personality lies in what the Bible calls 'fruits of the Spirit'. These are the traits that come as a consequence of having the Holy Spirit in our lives.

> *But the fruit of the Spirit is love, joy, peace, forbearance, kindness, goodness, faithfulness, gentleness and self-control. Against such things there is no law.*[144]

These attributes are part of the Spirit's personality. The more we have Him in our life, the more we will resemble Him. To gain a passion for the Spirit, we have to move from just knowing *about* Him to knowing Him.

3. Getting to Know His Gifts

> *Now to each one the manifestation of the Spirit is given for the common good. To one there is given through the Spirit a message of wisdom, to another a message of knowledge by means of the same Spirit, to another faith by the same Spirit, to another gifts of healing by that one Spirit, to*

---

[144] Galatians 5:22-23 NIV

> *another miraculous powers, to another prophecy, to another distinguishing between spirits, to another speaking in different kinds of tongues, and to still another the interpretation of tongues. All these are the work of one and the same Spirit, and he distributes them to each one, just as he determines.*[145]

The gifts of the Holy Spirit are carefully laid out for us by the Apostle Paul in his letter to the church in Corinth. Wisdom, knowledge, faith, healing, distinguishing between spirits, miraculous powers, prophecy, speaking in tongues and interpretation of tongues are all spiritual gifts from the Holy Spirit.

The first thing to note is the fact that these are, by their very nature, a benefit to us—hence gifts. The definition of a gift, by human standards is:

> *something given voluntarily without payment in return, as to show favor toward someone, honor an occasion, or make a gesture of assistance; present.*[146]

Or

> *a special ability or capacity; natural endowment; talent:*[147]

When the Holy Spirit gives us spiritual gifts, both of these

---

145 1 Corinthians 12:7-11 NIV
146 dictionary.com
147 dictionary.com

definitions come into play. It's God Himself showing us favor and honor—a special part of any significant relationship. And the gift itself involves the impartation of a special ability—we receive His gifts and become gifted. As we embrace receiving the Spirit's gifts throughout our life, our passion for Him will grow.

One of my love languages is gifts (much to my husband's dismay.) I love giving gifts, and I love receiving them. Some of my favorite moments in life with the people I love are occasions where gifts are given or received. These times build special memories of joy, and cultivate intimacy among family and friends. I believe the Holy Spirit loves giving gifts too, and I think that the process of *Him giving* and *us receiving* builds intimacy in our relationship with Him. We have our own special history with Him; occasions where He honors us with gifts. This, in-turn, cultivates a sense of being known and being parented.

The gifts He gives make us *gifted,* and our giftedness make us look more like Jesus. The more gifted we become, the more we reflect Christ which, in-turn, creates the propensity for us to fall in love with Him even more.

There's mystery behind getting these gifts because the Holy Spirit is the giver, and He will decide when and who to give to. We certainly can't earn them, since this defies the definition of a gift itself, but we can ask for them.

My daughter Penny came up to me the other day and said *"Mommy, I've got a great idea!"* "What's that?" I answered. *"I think we should go to the shop and you should buy me a present."* I couldn't stop smiling. How a 3 year old could figure out that the source of gifts comes from mummy's wallet, and the place to get them is the shop! But do you know what happened? I went to the shop and bought her a little gift. I had no intention that day of buying her anything, but she'd won me over with her cheekiness.

I think the Holy Spirit is delighted when we ask for His gifts. We don't know what gifts we'll get or in which season of life we'll receive them, but I think sometimes we can get them just because we've asked.

I ask for all His gifts all the time. I've received many of the gifts at different times of my life. Some have come for a season and some are with me all the time. I haven't always received the gifts I've asked for right away, but when they pop up later in life I wonder if my prayers back then are being answered in some way.

As a young Christian I was struck by the story of King Solomon asking for *"wisdom above all else"*. That was the first gift of the Spirit I asked for in prayer. I'm certainly not the wisest person in the world, but I've known times where in the midst of a crucial conversation, wisdom comes upon me and I have the right thing to say or right way to approach something.

I've known what it's like to carry an extraordinary amount of faith for a person or a project. This gift comes and goes in the ebb and flow of life. But when it's been there, I have a surprising capacity to pursue something impossible.

I strongly pursued the gift of healing for a long time. Healing is a gift that I cannot ignore, as I have an undeniable Godly hatred of sickness and disease. I've had times of incredible breakthrough and times where this gift seems distant, but I have the feeling that the gift of healing never goes away.

It's good to think about you're own experiences with receiving the gifts of the Spirit. For some of you this might be the first time you've even thought of them, for others you'll have your own unique journey.

As we get to know the Spirit Himself, it's crucial that we get to know His gifts. This is a part of our relationship with the Spirit that contains joy and great moments of celebration. The Holy Spirit wants us to experience the wonder and fascination that comes with these spiritual gifts.

Developing a passion for the Spirit comes by learning and experiencing His presence on a personal level. It's no good approaching Him from a distance where other's expressions of Him can blur who He is. It's no good getting to know about Him without getting to know Him as a person. This passion for Him comes from a place of intimacy—an everyday walk with God Himself.

For those of you who are hungry for more of the Holy Spirit, I will leave you with St Augustine's famous prayer.

> *Breathe in me, O Holy Spirit, that my thoughts may all be holy. Act in me, O Holy Spirit, that my work, too, may be holy. Draw my heart, O Holy Spirit, that I love but what is holy. Strengthen me, O Holy Spirit, to defend all that is*

holy. Guard me, then, O Holy Spirit, that I always may be holy. Amen.[148]

conclusion

The Word and The Spirit have each had their ambassadors throughout history; men, women and whole movements that have been thoroughly immersed in their teaching and have become their champions.

We've had incredible advances in the understanding of scripture. Gifted theologians such a A.W. Tozer and C.S. Lewis have brought a depth of clarity and insight to the written Word. The 21st Century has been blessed with articulate preachers who've brought revelatory application to scripture as well as some new Christian traditions that have encouraged the disciplines of reading the Bible.

There's been plenty of role models; people who exude a passion for Jesus and His good news. Evangelists like Billy Graham have focused the church on the power of the gospel. Churches like IHOP in Kansas embrace a night and day worship of the risen Jesus. The Antioch church planting movement has a vision statement saying "A passion for Jesus and His purposes on Earth."

Prophetic movements and key prophetic leaders have made huge strides forward in bringing an ease of use for the gift of prophecy for us normal Christians. Books, schools and online courses are available in ample supply for anyone interested in pursuing the now word of God. A 'prophetic etiquette' has also evolved that strives to put safeguards and accountability around prophecy

There are still swaths of people who have a hunger and passion for the Holy Spirit. The cry for the Holy Spirit's renewal is loud and clear—especially in younger generations who know a certain freedom from denominationalism. Today's Christians have an inheritance like none before. I believe it's in this day that heaven itself is calling, shouting even for the coming together of the Word and Spirit.

People of the Word need to get with the Spirit. People of the Spirit need to get into the Word. We need to forge a Holy Alliance by binding together what's been separated with unbreakable cords of love. Let's refuse division and spit it out. Let's fight for unity by reaching out for it.

For surely as we do, His Kingdom will come on Earth.